Made a Difference for That One

Made a Difference for That One

✦

A Surgeon's Letters Home from Iraq

Compiled by Meredith Coppola

iUniverse, Inc.
New York Lincoln Shanghai

Made a Difference for That One
A Surgeon's Letters Home from Iraq

Copyright © 2005 by Meredith Leigh Coppola

iUniverse books may be ordered through booksellers or by contacting:

iUniverse
2021 Pine Lake Road, Suite 100
Lincoln, NE 68512
www.iuniverse.com
1-800-Authors (1-800-288-4677)

ISBN-13: 978-0-595-36624-8 (pbk)
ISBN-13: 978-0-595-81053-6 (ebk)
ISBN-10: 0-595-36624-4 (pbk)
ISBN-10: 0-595-81053-5 (ebk)

Printed in the United States of America

This book is dedicated to the fine men and women who are serving, and have served, in the United States military, as well as their families at home.

"He who saves a single life is as if he had saved an entire world."

Mishna Sanhedrin 4:5

and

Qur'an 5:32

Contents

List of Illustrations

Foreword

On 18 January 2005, my husband, pediatric surgeon Major Christopher Paul Coppola, left our home in San Antonio, Texas for a four-month deployment in support of Operation Iraqi Freedom. In order to make our family separation a little easier, he decided to send home periodic updates, e-mails filled with information and stories about his life in a war zone.

Reading these letters, even a perfect stranger can get a pretty good idea of who Chris is. He loves good food (or bad food doused liberally with hot sauce), watching movies, gardening, and napping when and wherever possible. He has a nutty sense of humor, and loves being part of a great team, whether it be surgical or dodgeball. His writings convey his hope and humanity, as a surgeon, soldier, and citizen of the world. Most of all, Chris's abiding love for his family shines through. I suppose these are some of the more important facts to know about a person, but I thought you should also know how Chris came to be on that plane in January, the road he took to arrive at that moment.

Chris felt from a young age he wanted to be a physician; by the time he finished high school, he knew pediatric surgery was his calling. With this aim in mind, he attended Brown University, graduating with a Bachelor of Science in Biochemistry in 1990. It was in the fall of 1989 that joining the Air Force first became a possibility. Through the Health Professions Scholarship Program, Chris could be sworn in as a second lieutenant and perform four years of active duty service upon completion of his medical training. In return, the Air Force would pay for his education at the best medical school to accept him, Johns Hopkins University in Baltimore, Maryland. Chris and I became engaged shortly before he received his commission, and we had long talks about the risks and benefits of a military life, even if that life was 13 years in the future. In the end, the pros of serving his country (and graduating medical school debt-free!) outweighed any potential cons. We simply hoped and prayed the world would be at peace when it came Chris's time to serve.

After finishing Johns Hopkins in 1994, Chris completed a general surgery residency at Yale-New Haven Hospital in Connecticut. Upon receiving permission from the Air Force to pursue further specialty training, we were off to Children's

National Medical Center in Washington, DC, where Chris finally achieved his dream of becoming a pediatric surgeon in May 2003.

Up to this point in Chris's career, we had very little involvement with the military part of our lives. Aside from four months of training and service in medical school, his contact with the Air Force amounted to signing a big packet of forms once a year. Now, however, it was time for our family (including our three sons and a cat) to do our duty and report to San Antonio for a six-year commitment; two extra years had been added after the pediatric surgery fellowship. Wilford Hall Medical Center on Lackland Air Force Base is the Air Force's largest hospital, and patients come from installations around the world for treatment and care. As a pediatric surgeon, Chris tends to anyone under the age of 18 who needs surgical care, whether it be an accident victim, case of two am appendicitis, or an elective procedure. He loves working with children and their families, and his patients greatly appreciate his efforts on their behalf.

We had been in Texas just a little over a year when Chris found out he was going to Iraq. This was hard news for our family; Chris would be stationed at Balad Air Base, nicknamed Mortaritaville for the daily shellings by insurgents. My anxiety was running high, but I took some comfort in the fact he would not be doing much in-country traveling, and had promised me to always wear his armor and helmet when outdoors. Still, the time apart was unwelcome to say the least, and could not pass quickly enough. When we picked him up safe and sound at the San Antonio Airport 14 May 2005, it was one of the best days of my life.

As you will see, although Chris's main focus in Iraq was being a general surgeon for adults, he did find time and opportunity to utilize his specialized skills for helping Iraqi children. I know he will never forget any of the patients, young and old, who passed through his care during this time.

Chris Coppola is a proud soldier, caring physician, and loving son, father, and husband. We could ask for nothing more. I hope you will enjoy getting to know him through this book, his letters home.

Meredith Coppola
22 June 2005

1

"A Combat Landing"

Operation Iraqi Freedom, AORCENTAF
Friday, 21 JAN 2005

Dear Friends,

I would like to share a little bit of my deployment with you, and if time permits, will send updates in the future. If for any reason you don't want these emails cluttering your inbox, please let me know.

AORCENTAF stands for Area of Responsibility, United States Air Force Central Command. The Area of Responsibility is basically where the war is. Though the Global War on Terrorism and specifically Operation Iraqi Freedom involve personnel and resources around the globe, this area in general refers to Iraq and the surrounding countries. Central Command orchestrates the operational and tactical goings-on in this area, making the strategic goals set forth by Joint Chiefs of Staff a reality. In addition to the movement and activity of war fighters, Command controls support services for the marines, soldiers, airmen, and sailors over here. This involves, among other things, housing, food, and medical services, so for the next 120 days I belong to them.

In my life back home, I am an active duty military pediatric surgeon, caring for the minor dependents of the fighting men and women of the armed forces. Over here, I'm a trauma surgeon and a general surgeon. After all, that's why they keep me around, to support the war by patching up shot and blown up soldiers. That's why they paid for my medical school tuition and gave me a salary while I completed my two-year fellowship in pediatric surgery at the Children's National Medical Center in Washington D.C. Personally, I would rather be in Texas helping children with surgical emergencies or correcting birth defects. No doctor or father would want ever want to see their young countrymen and women in the grave danger of war. However, I know my duty, and I know where I belong when soldiers need help.

The journey out here started Tuesday and was a sweaty, tiring, two day affair. We reported at 10:30 for the 18:45 flight, so I got to take the Ben and Griffin to school and hang out with Reid on the deck. He will turn two-years-old while I am away. He doesn't know it and probably won't remember it, but I will. A father should be there for his son's birthdays. It seems wrong to have a job that keeps me away from such events. Home is where I belong. I can't wait to get back there!

I took a taxi in after saying goodbye to Meredith. She was so brave. We danced, she smiled, we kissed. There were no tears. My bags stowed in the back of the taxi, I grabbed the passenger door handle and paused. I ran back to our front door for just one more kiss before leaving. I opened the door to find her crying, and that got me going too. I tried to keep smiling. We held each other so tight I thought my ribs would break. This is the longest I would be away from this wonderful woman since we married July 13th 1991. It was unimaginable. I was taking a taxi because I thought that would be safer than either of us driving on that day.

At the base, I thought I had been pretty efficient until I reached my hand in my pocket and realized I still had Meredith's car keys! If that was the worst to go wrong with my departure, it would be no big deal. Turned out we had a use for the extra keys we had made. I called Meredith to laugh about the mistake, and then slipped the keys into a package and mailed them home from the base post office.

The day was a snail-paced trail from briefing to briefing. At least everyone had turned up. We were excited, expectant, worried, and ambivalent. I wasn't surprised that we were told to report eight full hours before our departure time.

That's worse than the security delay for an international flight at Baltimore-Washington International Airport! It's par for the course to keep alive the hallowed military tradition of "hurry up and wait". Volunteers had come to the hospital to feed our nerves with coffee and sweet cakes. All around me my colleagues were kissing their sweethearts and babies goodbye. Our hospital commander, the general, came out to see us off. He and one of the colonels stopped me to say hello. "Good morning, Sir, good morning Ma'am," I addressed them, suddenly aware of how long my hair had gotten during the past two weeks while I was trying to spend as much time as possible with my family. "Does he know yet?" the general asked. "No," she replied, "the list doesn't come out until next week." They told me I had been selected for promotion. I wasn't supposed to know yet, but they figured it was okay to break the news early since I was skipping out of the country. My surgery commander was there as well. "Coppola, get your hair cut!" he admonished, grinning at me, and then wished us all safe journey. So there I was, still smiling after four hours of waiting and being briefed. Finally, at 18:00 we loaded into a bus and rode over to the charter flight leaving from Kelly Airport. It was strange to just walk onto the airplane, no x-ray or pat-down, after having grown accustomed to the usual security walk for civilian flights. It was just as comfortable—I mean cramped—as a civilian flight. The crews were very nice to us and we were fed constantly, even if it was just airplane food. It's a good thing because we spent the next 20 hours on that plane with only two short stops. The first was in Baltimore, and when I stepped out for a breath of air, it was cold! We picked up a lot of other deploying troops in Baltimore and continued on. On the overhead compartments there was artwork from children with all sorts of encouraging messages. One that stands out in my memory depicted assorted forces engaging the enemy in a heated battle. Stick-figure soldiers were fearlessly leaping from the belly of a plane spewing fire. Paratroopers with chutes unfurled shouldered weapons and pulled off rounds at the ground. In the center, a massive tank flying a creative rendition of the "Stars and Bars" was emblazoned on the side with "USa! rocks" (sic). Printed on the side vertically was "God bless you!" I have my suspicions it was drawn by a boy, but that's just a guess.

The next stop was a chance to stretch our legs in Shannon, Ireland. My first visit to Ireland! As you'd expect, I saw nothing but the terminal. Fortunately, there was a pub! That dark, thick pint of stout will have to be my last taste of fermented craft for four months, since alcohol is not allowed in the Area of Responsibility.

After another six-hour flight, we landed at Al-Udeid in Qatar. It was covered in an inch of water and two inches of fine silt and mud under that. But it blended in perfectly with our desert camouflage uniforms, so at least the military fashion consultants had chosen well. Of course my woodland green armor was a different matter. Mobility had run out of desert armor, but I suppose for armor, the color doesn't matter as much as how hard it is. I took a short tour of the base with some of the other doctors, but we didn't have to go far to learn there wasn't much to see. Happily, we did find the dining facility. As we ate our hot breakfast, we watched preparations for President Bush's second inauguration on the wide-screen TV. I guess I'd rather be at a high-priced party in Washington, but after 20 hours on a plane that meal couldn't have tasted better.

For the next leg of the journey to our hospital at Balad Airbase, we loaded into a C-130 military transport plane. We sat facing each other in web netting seats with our gear hanging all around. The pilot made a "combat landing", which is a quick drop to the runway from a high altitude after a few maneuvers to the right and left. It actually was a lot smoother than it sounds. Besides my joints getting a little stiff, it was relatively comfortable. After we landed, the back of the plane opened again to form a ramp. The crew rolled all of our cargo down the ramp on a big pallet.

So finally we were at LSA Anaconda. LSA stands for Logistics Support Area. My new base is one of the supply centers for many smaller posts in the area. Additionally, with two long runways and as the site of Saddam Hussein's former Air Force Academy, it is a capable arrival and departure point for many of the flights in and out of Iraq. It took a lot of trudging through mud to pick up our bags and move to the lodging facility and it was 23:00 when I was let into my room with its cozy cot.

The housing looks a lot like a trailer park except there are no pink flamingos and the walls are sandbagged. Our homes were trailers, divided into two or three sections, with thin wood-paneled walls dividing the rooms. Some of us had singles while more junior troops shared a room. Officers more senior than I had a wet trailer with an indoor bathroom and shower, while the rest of us walked to port-a-potties. At the moment the night was cold and damp, but each trailer had an air conditioning unit which I knew would come in handy in the hot months to come.

And so, after a long journey, I got out my clippers and got my shaggy head groomed. A nice warm shower also felt great. I stopped by the dining facility for a bite at midnight chow before turning in. I crashed hard on my cot and quickly fell asleep. Dreams of Meredith and the boys filled my tired head. I hope you all are well and I already miss home very much. Take good care of yourselves, and I can't wait to see you again. I'll write again soon and let you know how things go at the hospital.

Warmest Regards,

Chris

2

"American Soldiers' Blood"

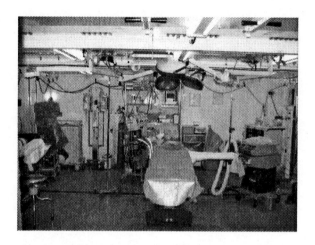

Air Force Theater Hospital, Balad, Iraq
Monday, 24 JAN 2005

Dear Friends,

I've got a few minutes before the morning's cases start, so I wanted to take a moment to send an update. Even though it has only been a few days, it seems like a lot has happened. I had my first call day and we cared for some casualties, so I've been initiated.

As I walked through the base, I realized that every building here looks like the same hastily cobbled square of concrete surrounding a tent or a box, surrounded by the same reddish-brown mud. So the view is pretty boring! But within each nondescript tent or box, we have transported from the United States the ability to do some function as closely as possible as we do it at home.

The hospital, although no departure from this architecture, is an impressive structure. The cement walls surrounding the multiple tents that make up the hos-

6

pital are about 16 feet high. Some exposures of the hospital are lined by bunkers, which are a double wall of cement with a cement roof so you can walk inside them like a tunnel. At the entrance to the hospital compound is a guard post. There is a turnpike-style lift gate that spans the gap between the cement walls and the chain-link fence topped with barbed wire. The guard doesn't use the gate, but lifts and lowers a heavy steel cable to let vehicles and pedestrians pass.

There is a corridor outside the entrance to the ER. It is surfaced in—you guessed it—cement, and covered for part of its length with a tin roof. Patients come from the helipad beside the hospital and enter the ER tent along this corridor. Rows of NATO stretchers and the two-wheeled frames that allow these stretchers to be rolled from place to place are stacked up outside the ER, ready and waiting for incoming injured.

Continuing our tour, once inside the ER you are greeted by the friendly staff, from the US and Australia. The ER is a long tent with three stretchers on each side, ready for walk-in patients. The half of the ER farthest from the entrance has no stretchers, and is always kept open for emergent patients, rolling in after they are unloaded from the helicopters. Four seriously injured patients can be treated at once. The present quiet while this trauma area is empty gives no clue of the whirlwind of efficient activity that goes on when patients arrive.

Continuing out the rear exit of the ER tent, you enter the PLX, or Pharmacy, Laboratory, and X-ray area. We prefer to call it the surgeons' area, because that is where we hang out. The hospital is set up for the surgeons' maximal convenience and function. Everything flows right through our area. We have a few desks and computers to check on messages from other bases as well as x-ray results. For patients awaiting their prescriptions, there are a few soft black couches finished in faux leather. At night, those couches double as our call room, where we might get a chance to lay down in between patients. If anything should occur, we are right where we need to be to respond to the action.

Next is the OR. Looks like any OR, but don't forget it has been transported to Iraq in pieces and lets us bring modern care just miles away from where people are getting hurt. The OR differs from most of the hospital in that it is a hard metal container. It is much like operating in a box. It is the size of about half the container on the back of a tractor trailer. As you look around, you can see hinges and braces where the walls were folded out like an RV living area. Lights are mounted on the ceiling and there is a standard operating table in the center of the room. Off to the left is a second operating table so we can operate on two patients at once in the same room should the need arise. This OR is one of three so we can perform six emergency operations simultaneously.

One of the people I get to work with is neurosurgeon Lee. He saved a two-year-old boy's life last night. The boy had a bullet fragment enter his forehead and cause bleeding in his brain. I helped Lee open the boy's skull and relieve the pressure on his brain. It's not something I would have gotten to do at home. Here in Iraq, we don't have the residents and medical students we are used to. Usually we would have their help on our cases. In their absence, we are stepping out of our usual specialties and helping each other out.

That same night I took care of some Iraqi National Guard soldiers who had been shot. One would have bled to death had this hospital not been here. When we needed more blood during the operation, at 03:00 no less, an announcement went out over the base for blood donors. Within 45 minutes, we had a unit of blood from an American soldier and seven more to follow.

At one end of the hospital is the MWR (Morale, Welfare, and Recreation) tent. It's a place for the recuperating soldiers to relax and find something to take their minds off their surroundings. There are movies, books, satellite TV, and running water on the floor since it has been raining like crazy here. This is where I am right now, plugged into the Internet sending this message home.

Back in my hooch (that's what we call our trailers), I'm starting to feel a little more at home. When I reflect on the fact that we are in the middle of a war and some troops are out there with no roof over their heads, it is luxury beyond my wildest dreams. Before leaving home, my sons Ben and Griffin each gave me one of their toys to keep safe for them through my travels. So my foreign surrounds seem a little less alien with Griffin's Shrek and Ben's baseball right next to where I sleep. I haven't quite unpacked fully, probably won't ever.

I hope you all are well, and loving life! I'm doing fine over here. Even though I can't wait to get back and I am already counting days, I hope I can help a few people out. Pray for peace and a rapid return home for our countrymen in harm's way.

Take good care of yourselves,

Chris

3

"Greetings from Sunny Balad!"

Air Force Theater Hospital 332 EMDG Balad, Iraq
Thursday, 27 JAN 2005

Dear Friends,

I hope this email finds you well. I have appreciated your emails so much. It is like a ray of sunshine through the mud to receive word from home. I miss you all very much and the time until I can return home is trickling by. Already I am 5% done! Not much so far. I don't know much, but I do know this, you can't stop the clock.

I told you a bit about the hospital interior, but it is easier to describe viewing it from the outside. Our tent hospital was built on a largely empty lot. The only remaining structure on the land from its days under Saddam's reign is a small pillbox building with a bedroom, bathroom, living area, and laundry. We don't know who used it back then, but it seems like it would be a comfortable little bachelor's apartment. The top of the building offers a good panoramic view of the hospital from a small height. The hospital is modular and increased in size by adding on more tents. In addition to being able to operate on six patients simultaneously, we have room for 80 patients to recover in the wards. The hospital is two rows of tents, connected by corridors. Specialized areas like the operating rooms and radiology are in steel containers. Everything is on one level, and you can walk to every area without having to brave the rain or heat outside. After a few days time providing modern medical care in these tents, it has been easy to forget I'm not in a brick and mortar hospital. There are very few things I want for in the care of my patients. I think this is partly because our corps has been willing to stretch the limits of our capabilities and pitch in more than we do at home. We have started our deployment eager to do whatever we can to help the troops.

I have been somewhat busy with operations. Over the past few days we have received some men injured in ambushes, improvised explosive device (IED) attacks, and one accident where a troop transport called a Bradley Fighting Vehicle flipped over into water. When we care for Americans, they usually undergo one operation here, are then flown to the U.S. base in Germany, and travel on to the United States to complete their recovery. Most soldiers are back in the United States one or two days after being injured. The Iraqis I treat will stay in this hospital until they are well enough to go home. Many of them will have multiple operations before they can leave.

I have fast grown to depend on my fine colleagues to work as an effective team. The stress and austerity of the environment adds to a spirit of cooperation and interdependence. We usually work with two or more surgeons in each operation and we quickly finish one case and move onto the next. Yesterday during our operation we received warning to put on our protective gear. It made for interesting operative attire. Surgeon Brett, from Hawaii, and anesthetist Annie were with me in the operating room. It was so strange to look up from my work and see them wearing camouflaged armored vests and helmets over the pale blue of the scrub suits traditionally worn. In spite of the increased threat of attack during this period of alarm red, we continued with our work as if this was any other operation. The All Clear signal was sounded without incident.

The little boy who needed brain surgery after the gunshot wound to his head has left the hospital. We were very relieved to hear that his parents had also both survived the incident. After he began to recover he was very active, up and out of bed and wild like a normal little two-year-old boy. It was a bright point on rounds to visit him and celebrate his survival. Amazingly, a toddler's brain can remodel and shift functions from the damaged portion to normal portions. An adult's brain would not be able to recover as easily, if at all.

We had some fun discovering that 26 JAN is Australia Day, commemorating the day of European colonization. The Australian nurses and doctors warned us they might be acting a bit strangely to honor the day. Having witnessed their everyday behavior, I assured them we probably wouldn't notice anything out of the ordinary. One of the nurses from the intensive care unit was proudly displaying his national colors on his forehead. It is an international experience participating in this medical venture. The Australians form a good portion of our staff. They welcomed us here our first night, and some actually helped us carry our bags. We have received British and Croatian casualties, and many of our patients are Iraqi National Guardsmen or policemen. People of all nationalities work as contractors throughout the base. This situation is obviously monitored very closely for security concerns.

I'm sure I've mentioned that one of my favorite pastimes here has become eating, frequently and in high volumes! I thought I'd take you on a tour of the fine establishments I have discovered. There are four dining facilities, or DFACs, on the base. The one closest to us is DFAC2. It is two blocks down the road from our hooches and the hospital. The DFAC is a series of prefabricated buildings made of corrugated steel, further protected by an outer ring of cement blast walls. The cement walls and bunkers have been painted with various units' emblems, flags, and leaders' names. Some are patriotic, with bold eagles and flowing United States flags, while others are whimsical with heavily armed bulldogs or dragons. The DFAC is also where I can drop off my mail. There is a standard mailbox chained to one of the blast walls. The gravel lot is vacant most hours, but when mealtime arrives, people come out of the woodwork and stream to the entrances.

On the way in, you pass your friendly DFAC guard, who checks your ID and makes sure you aren't carrying a backpack. That's not to keep you from bringing food out—we are allowed to do that—it's for safety. At another base an attack on a dining facility was accomplished by smuggling in explosives. The guards keep a close eye on all the troops, contractors, and local nationals who gather to eat. Next, we all wash our hands. You build up a lot of grime on your hands because everything here is coated with a fine layer of dust. The stainless steel sinks in the vestibule of the dining facility are all topped with big yellow bottles of "Fairy" brand soap. Our mothers would be so proud of us washing our hands before dinner. There is always hot chow, morning, noon, and night. And then there is my favorite, midnight chow. We usually have a choice of two hot entrees, such as Salisbury steak or breaded veal. Often the two choices seem like the same meat and filler substance but with a different coating or sauce so you can tell them apart. I find myself asking questions like, "Excuse me, is that pork or turkey?"

There is also the grill if you need a quick fix of hamburgers or fries. Then we all sit down to dig in while we watch the news or a movie on the big screen, brought to us via satellite transmission from Armed Forces Network. There are many beverage choices, and I usually bring a few bottles of Gatorade home. After dinner, we get ice cream!

Sometimes I can't get out of the hospital to eat, so I go to the little mess tent on site. I'm a regular there for breakfast since we start rounds early. The line forms fast the instant the tent flap opens. It's not pretty, but you can grab a quick bite and get back to work. Like any hospital, we run on coffee which is available all night long.

Well, I hear a helicopter dusting off the helipad, so I'd better get going to see who has come in. Until next time, I hope you all are having fun and loving life! As you might guess, life is varied and unpredictable in Balad. Just today, surgeon Brian and I found ourselves painting the walls of the little pillbox building so we could move in and make it our call room. We never know what we might be doing from one day to the next. God bless you and keep you safe.

Warm regards,

Chris

P.S. Many have asked, "What can we send and what can we do for the troops?" We are very well-equipped and supplied. Here at the hospital, I have access to more than most troops so I personally don't have a need for anything material. I would love the capacity to do laparoscopic surgery over here, but I guess that is just a luxury in a war zone. I suppose it would be nice to have some varieties of hot sauces to drown the food. We have a good supply of ketchup, Heinz 57 and Tabasco sauce (which even comes in the Meals Ready to Eat (MRE) in a miniature bottle), but that means we can disguise the food in only three flavors. I have ready access to a phone, but I'm sure any troop would appreciate a pre-paid phone calling card to use when they get their rare access to a phone. Those looking to help could search on-line for ideas at the Red Cross or www.anysoldier.com. Of course, continue to exercise your rights to our great freedom and make sure you inform your congressperson of how you feel about the war and how you would like to support the troops. As a doctor, I think the best support of the troops would be to get them home and out of the way of the bullets and explosions. But most of all, what I would ask you to do for all of us is to offer your prayers and good wishes for our safety, continued strength, and inspiration to continue to our duty the best we can and make our country proud. Be safe, take care, and love life.

4

"Election Day"

Balad AB, Iraq
Sunday, 30 JAN 2004

Dear Friends,

Today are the first free Iraqi elections since Saddam Hussein was removed from power. We have been alternating time glued to the CNN broadcast and taking care of the casualties coming in. Last night a few American soldiers were admitted and will be quickly airlifted out to Germany. Polls opened at 08:00, and since then we have seen a trickling of Iraqi civilian casualties from the many mortars, suicide bombings, and improvised explosive devices (IED) directed at the polling stations.

We are about to operate on a seven-year-old boy who accompanied his father to vote. They were 100 feet from the polling place when there was an explosion and a fragment hit the boy in the head, fracturing his skull. Luckily, his brain seems okay and hopefully he will recover with his faculties intact. We are also taking care of a 17-year-old girl who was shot in the neck, and an elderly woman with multiple fragment injuries to her legs. They are certainly not people who deserve to be a victim of war. There is no justice in these events.

Without giving away anything specific, I want to tell you about some of the preparations we have made for the elections. We have minimized activities with mass gatherings and put a hold on recreational activities. Many of the creature comforts of the base, such as the gym, theater, and Post Exchange are closed today. We are wearing armor at all times and traveling in pairs. Surgeon Brian and I are hanging out in the hospital in our "battle rattle", as we call the Kevlar helmet and the Kevlar vest with ceramic plates in front and back. Together, these items weigh 35 pounds.

The perimeter is well-guarded, and there are constant patrols. The chain-link fence with razor wire isn't so imposing, but the watchtowers are serious. They are draped in breakup netting and manned with sharpshooters. There is a zone around the base which is kept clear. Off in the distance, I can see the minaret of one of the mosques of Balad city. It is a blue tipped tiny tower next to the shorter, but larger, blue dome of the mosque itself. Often we see shepherds, children, goats, and sheep grazing in the fields outside the fence. Since most of the shepherds are children, I guess you could describe it as kids watching kids. All entry points to the base are heavily guarded. Before I arrived there was a suicide bombing at the gate closest to the hospital, but the multiple layers of security prevented that attack from breaching the perimeter. We are still caring for one of the brave Iraqi guards injured in the attempt.

We all wear identification and minimize activity that would make us easy targets. Perhaps the most important component of being secure is an attitude of vigilance. This base, with its thousands of service members, has thousands of pairs of eyes watching for anything out of the ordinary. I am very appreciative of the brave men and women whose job it is to make sure I can do my work in safety every day. You might worry that there would be accidents with so many young people walking around heavily armed. It is impressive to see how respectful people are of the deadly force they command. Simple safety measures, such as a reinforced barrel to clear your weapon at the entrance to dining facilities and the hospital, keep us in strict routines so we don't hurt ourselves.

On the other hand, putting a weapon in my hands is a dubious prospect. Wisely, we doctors are under even stricter restrictions with our arms and ammunition, but I'm trained and ready. Even though I'm a bit uncomfortable carrying a gun, I chin up and go about the business of being a doctor. Many of our structures are sandbagged and reinforced to withstand minor blasts. It is true that we occasionally receive mortar or rocket fire, but it is very inaccurate, and often the 40-year-old shells the bad guys (if they are firing at me and my patients, they are bad guys) launch don't even detonate. That's what the unexploded ordnance crew tells us, anyway! Besides the sandbags, we are also protected by the cement walls I've described. I'm telling you all about our layers of security (even if only vaguely) mainly because I don't want you to worry about us. We will do our job and face the risk. And when my job is done, I will get the heck out of here, but fast!

I know I am witnessing history as I watch the bravery and spirit of the Iraqis who are coming out in droves to vote. Beyond the hollow threats of weapons of mass destruction and links to Al-Qaeda, seeing this great thing happen makes even a cynical critic of the war like me hopeful. Even if this war was started for the wrong reasons and young American troops have suffered for it, I will be the first to embrace a positive result. As I watch the reports of suicide bombers and attacks on voters in Baghdad and Mosul, I am praying and wishing for their safety. We stand ready to help anyone hurt in the process. The danger the Iraqis are facing as they exercise a right that we take for granted points out how blessed we are to live free. Our country may need to better learn how to cooperate with international institutions, but we sure do know how to live.

Well, enough of my yakkin'! You all take care and have a great day wherever you are in the world. But first, pause and give much respect to the brave Iraqi people as they step out and make a stand. Be well, have fun, and love life!

Your man in Balad,

Chris

5

"Meal, Ready to Eat"

Surgeons' Call Building
Thursday, 3 FEB 2005

Thank you kindly for the emails I have received. It is so helpful to have words of encouragement from back home. Also, when I get a little bit of news, I don't feel so isolated from the people I know and love.

As you know, the Iraqi elections, although marred by scattered—and I think desperate—occurrences of violence, were very successful. Today I was able to catch a rebroadcast of the State of the Union address, and I was moved by the presence of the Iraqi woman who braved the sound of mortars to go out with her family and vote. Like you all, I was also greatly affected by the presence of the parents of the Marine killed in Fallujah. I do feel I am a part of a great process, even if there may be a stutter step from time to time along the way. I will continue to pray for peace as well as the promise of freedom for all people, but

17

guided by the wisdom to find this freedom with the least human suffering and loss of life.

Today I get the chance to take a breather after a 24-hour shift on call as the SOD, or Surgeon on Duty. This is the same term used for the surgical resident on duty at the Veterans' Administration Hospital in West Haven, CT. My friend and mentor, Professor Irvin, used to call it the "sorry sod". I was able to spend most of the evening leisurely checking on postoperative patients or napping. In the wee hours, "dustoff" (arrival of medical transport) at the helipad brought two Marines injured in an ambush south of our position. My colleague, dentist Dave, took care of the first young man's facial injuries, while I called in my backup, surgeon Mike, so we could explore and clean the neck wounds of the second. When this brave Marine woke up, I asked him if he was in any pain. He turned to me, shrugged and said, "No, but I really gotta' pee." If I should ever so narrowly escape death, I'm sure I would be a quivering wreck!

But first, if I could step back a bit in time, yesterday we had some afternoon cases that took us through until the evening. Since I was the SOD, I couldn't leave the hospital to visit the DFAC (dining facility). The guys, of course, offered to bring me back something good to eat, but I declined politely because I thought there were still a few hot dinners left in the hospital cafeteria. However, once I got there, all I found was some Gatorade and MRE's. Those of you who know need no further explanation. For those of you who don't know, words cannot fully express the reality of MRE's. That difficulty won't stop me from trying to explain!

MRE stands for "Meal, Ready-to-Eat", and I sure was ready to eat after a full day of operations. MRE's can be shipped, trucked, dropped from a plane, left in the hot, cold or wet, and are a soldier's primary foodstuff when he is out of garrison. I don't know the shelf life, but it's long. Not as long as C-rations, but no one in their right mind would even consider eating those anymore. The last time I had eaten an MRE was during my HPOIC (Health Professions Officer Indoctrination Course), or as I like to call it, fake boot camp. Since then, there have been all sorts of space-age improvements to the MRE, most significantly the heater pack.

I scurried away to our new call room, which was a former above ground bunker when our base belonged to the Iraqi Air Force under Saddam Hussein. We surgeons had commandeered the structure and stocked it with every creature comfort we could lay our hands on. With a pager on my belt and a two-way radio at my side, I was ready for a dinner adventure. I started by breaking open the package and spreading out the contents. I had chosen Menu #9 Beef Stew, because I thought stew left a wide margin of error in preparation and safety. I'm saving grilled beef patties and chicken enchiladas for when I am signed off on the basics.

I started with something familiar, crackers and grape jelly. The crackers were a bit dry and brittle. The jelly was a sweet and wholesome reminder of all things American. Emboldened by this success, I moved onto the more challenging main course. The food comes in a foil-lined pouch within a slim cardboard sleeve. The MRE heater is a mystery to me. You simply open the plastic bag, pour water on the filter packet of ominous-looking chemical powder, and presto! You've got a hot meal. I took time to read the rather lengthy warning label on the heater. If the military could tell me, "Don't worry, just take it!" about the anthrax vaccine, but required a paragraph to warn me about the heater, it must be darn close to a weapon of mass destruction. "Vapor released contains hydrogen gas." Could this be the answer to the energy crisis? "No open flame." Then why did they include a pack of matches in the MRE? Don't they understand guys like to burn stuff, especially stuff we're told not to burn? "If more than ten MRE heaters are used in a vehicle or enclosed space, ventilation is required." Being crammed into an unventilated space with too many of your mates describes approximately 75% of military life and all mealtimes. Best of all: "Do not use the water from the MRE heater for consumption." I'm scared to breathe the vapor coming from the heater, so I'm not about to go using it as a teabag!

Unfortunately, I only read the first step of the instructions, "Add water to double line on bag." I say unfortunately because soon after that the heater got too hot to hold and I had to hastily cram it into the box with the pouch of beef stew without reading the rest. Actually, I'm proud I read even the first step of the directions. That's further than I usually get with instructions before trying it on my own. The box stated that my MRE would give me energy for top performance. It went on to inform me that I need three meals each day in field and the MRE provided 1200-1300 calories. I was advised to eat the high carbohydrate items first, such as the crackers. See, who needs directions!

While the stew was warming, I mixed up my chocolate dairy-shake in its own pouch with six ounces of water and scarfed it down. Yummy, tasted like runny chocolate mousse. I slid the heater out of the cardboard sleeve (it was Africa hot), and read enough of the directions to realize I had folded it wrong. I corrected the situation by folding it properly and tilting the box up on two new books I had received in awesome care packages earlier that day. While waiting for the stew to finish in my tiny kitchen, I opened what I thought was a napkin and found squares of tissue. Either my military benefactors wanted me to refrain from wiping my nose on my sleeve, or they were predicting I would be in need of tissue squares after eating my tasty MRE.

The warmed pouch felt comforting and eerily alive. As instructed, I kneaded it to distribute the temperature evenly, but felt like I was crushing my potatoes. I tore open the packet greedily and sampled the nourishing contents. Like everything served here, it required the zest and camouflage of hot sauce, so I was happy to find a miniature bottle of Tabasco sauce right when I needed it! (Speaking of which, I am very excited that at this minute a crate of "Foo's Fire" hot sauce is making its way from California to Balad, possibly on the back of a camel!) I cleaned the pouch out and moved on to dessert. "Cookies with pan coated chocolate discs" sounded suspicious. I'm surprised it wasn't an acronym, like "cookies with PACHODS". There was no need to be cryptic; PACHODS are Government Issue M&M's. The cookies were not what I would call "good". A better description would be "rock-hard with a vague aftertaste of soap". The Chiclets-like gum wasn't much better, resembling mint-impregnated chunks of partially cured clay. Still, the meal had its intended effect, and I soon collapsed fast asleep on the couch with a full belly. Taking a page from a more experienced MRE-eater in our corps, I later created a postcard by cutting out a panel from the cardboard box in which the stew was packed. It is now on its way to my boys, marked "Free!" where the stamp goes, like all my mail. Thanks, Uncle Sam!

So with that meal and a bit of sleep, I was hard-charging and ready to go when the injured Marines arrived early this morning. I thank God they are both doing very well so far and by tonight should be on a transport flight to Germany, the first leg of their journey home to a well-earned hero's rest.

When the cavalry arrived for morning rounds to relieve me, I made my way back home to the trailers (which, by the way, are on Black Jack Boulevard, a great street for a fan of Atlantic City like me). After a shower and change to a fresh uniform, I picked up clean clothes at the free laundry, which is staffed by some very nice Filipino ladies. I asked the one at the counter for a picture with me. When I showed it to her on the camera she looked up and said triumphantly, "I am beautiful!" Friendly faces and Haliburton-supplied support staff make the chores of living easier, but they don't make me miss home any less. I know I have no right to complain. I am so fortunate to be useful here. Still, I will count the days until I am in the arms of my family again. For now, take care and God bless.

Faithfully submitted,

Chris

6

"Commander's Call"

Housing Area 4 Hooch A9, Iraq
Tuesday, 8 FEB 2005

Dear Friends,

I hope all is well with you. We are doing fine here in Iraq. It's a bit late, and I have to rise early tomorrow for my on-call day. Before passing out, I want to set down a few thoughts for the day. How was the Superbowl back home? I was very pleased to hear the Pats took it. I attempted to watch the game, but I didn't have the stamina. You see, here it started at 02:30. I went to the hospital morale tent for the Superbowl party, and many troops were relaxing around the big screen TV. We were watching comedy, playing cards and ping-pong, and sipping Beck's beer—the non-alcoholic kind, that is. The party started at 8pm; I was able to make it to 11pm, when I showed my age and hit the rack. The rack, of course, is wherever you go horizontal to catch some sleep. Like medical training, the military lives by the words "eat when you can, sleep when you can."

I headed home from the hospital. As I reported last time, I live along Black Jack Boulevard; however, after a Humvee had a close encounter with the street sign, "Black" was broken off and "Jack" was left, so it would seem that I now live on Jack Boulevard. My bunk had been sagging like a hammock over uncomfortable crossbars after being put through the abuse of many troops (before my stay in Balad, not during, if I might clarify). I had resorted to sleeping on a cot, but the housing staff finally put some plywood under my mattress which made for a luxurious bunk. Some of the hard-charging younger fellows in our corps stuck it out to the end of the Superbowl and then came straight to work. I just can't do that anymore! They did their jobs well today, but the fatigue showed in their eyes. I guess some things are just worth the pain.

I was glad for the extra sleep Sunday night, considering what Monday was to bring. In the past few weeks, we had run drills to prepare for a MASCAL, or "Mass Casualty" event. That is when a high number of patients arrive together and the resources of the hospital become overwhelmed. Those drills paid off today because we received seven patients in quick succession and nearly all of them required an operation. CNN reported that 26 individuals were killed today when two police stations were attacked with explosives. Our hospital received many of the policemen injured in Baqubah, where a graduation ceremony for new Iraqi police officers was targeted with explosives. A call was put out to all surgeons to return to the hospital. I had changed into PT (physical training) gear and was just headed out for exercise, but I hoofed it into the hospital without taking time to change. One Black Hawk helicopter had already landed and a second was approaching for dustoff.

All patients come through the ER. Patients are triaged upon arrival so they can be ranked in order of the severity of their illness. Our flight commander, surgeon Dave, was the trauma czar. He stood in the middle of the action. We all pitched in to help and reported our findings to surgeon Dave. He assigned tasks for personnel to perform on patients, and governed their flow into the operating room.

With the neurosurgeons, I took a patient who had received injuries to his head and legs to one of the operating rooms. I again had no time to change out of PT gear, so I scrubbed in and gowned as I was, waterproof booties on my shoes to contain the thick, brown, gravel-encrusted mud that clings to our boots wherever we go. Surgeon Brian scrubbed in to help me control the bleeding and clean the wounds in the man's leg. As we worked to save this severely injured man, I considered what a weighty decision it must be to become a police officer in today's Iraq. Perhaps these young men have few other choices for employment as the country recovers from the damages of war. Maybe it is a desire to have a front-line job in rebuilding their country. Either way, it is clear that attacks by the insurgents are bringing suffering mostly to the Iraqi people themselves.

After moving our patient to the intensive care unit, I received another young policeman who had been burned over nearly half of his body. Urologist Eddie, who had come in to check any injuries below the belt, stayed to help me finish cleaning and dressing the patient's burns. It was just one of many examples of troops doing work outside of their usual scope of function. Everyone tried to pitch in wherever their efforts were needed. At one point, we had so many operations occurring at once that two patients underwent surgery in the same room, just as we had rehearsed in our drills.

As the last patients' operations were completed and they were tucked into the wards, the hospital quieted down. The nursing teams continued their care into the night. This was not a very large mass casualty event at all, but the team had pulled together smoothly. There were no complaints or bickering and everyone stepped forward to give of their efforts and skills. This brings me to the real reason I wanted to write to you.

Before the election, our commander, surgeon Chuck, summoned us together for a Commander's Call. We are still a green team, just starting to feel comfortable with our hospital as well as the ins and outs of our base. He gave a brief talk that was both calming and inspiring. I thought his words demonstrated his strong character and leadership ability. My trust in his integrity gives me a feeling of security. I will try to convey the spirit of his heartening message.

He called on us to consider the eagle, a symbol emblazoned on our crest. He likened the head of the eagle to God, guiding our purpose. He described the wings of the eagle as freedom and democracy, and the talons as courage and sacrifice. He told us he had seen courage in our ranks as we worked efficiently under the threat of attack, and he knew of the many sacrifices made by us and our families. He warned us that during the election we may be called upon to treat seriously injured people. He described to us the spirit he had seen in patients he had treated as a reconstructive surgeon, and how months afterward they told him the trial had made them stronger. Lastly, he reminded us that when injured troops come our way, they will not be seeking our sympathy, but will need our help. It is our duty to provide that help without fear or hesitation. As you can see by these strong sentiments, we are in good hands.

I will end this note with a tiny request. We have a small artificial Christmas tree in the surgeons' area that we call the holiday tree. It is now decorated blue and white for the January winter back home. We have failed in our task to decorate it for February to honor Valentine's Day, but perhaps we will do better for March. If any of you have St. Patrick's Day decorations you can spare, please send them to us in Iraq!

Now I'm off to bed for a few hours so I can deliver the goods again tomorrow. I am thankful for the people back home whom I miss dearly, and I pray for peace, a quick recovery for our patients, and a safe return home for our team. Be well, have fun, and love life!

Your man in Balad,

Chris

7

"To Know And to Act, One And the Same"

LSA Anaconda, Balad, Iraq
Sunday, 13 FEB 2003

Dear Friends,

   I'm not on call tonight, I've got no operations to do, and it is Sunday. By Sunday, I mean the wee hours of Sunday, as in 01:00. I've retired to my room, and it is good to be idle and alone. Pretty soon, it's going to be good to be asleep! The days do run together here. It is the same routine day in, day out. It is hard to know what day it is. I have called Meredith at home too early on a Saturday morning, mistakenly thinking it was a school day and she was getting the boys ready for the bus. We joke that it feels like the movie *Groundhog Day*, in which the same day repeats endlessly.

In order to break up the routine a little, we have tried to make Sundays just a tiny bit different. We reduced the number of scheduled cases to a minimum to strive for a day of rest. We used to start rounds an hour later than usual at 08:30, but the night shift requested we keep the earlier time. Imagine having finished a 12-hour shift, and then being asked to hang around the hospital for an additional hour just to wait for the surgeons to show up. It was quickly changed back to 07:30. We also do not have scheduled meetings on Sundays. Some people worship on Sunday at one of the three base chapels. If we end up with some free time, on Sundays or otherwise, we cannot go far, but Camp Anaconda does offer a few choices for diversion.

Tonight I visited neurosurgeon Lee in his hooch to watch the movie *Napoleon Dynamite*. I like to tell Meredith when I have seen a new movie, and then she can see it. That way when she sees it, we can talk about it, and it will be like we saw it together. Lee had a few troops over. Before the movie we watched episode seven of *Band of Brothers*, which was a riveting account of the siege on the town of Foy after the Battle of the Bulge. And before that, Lee and therapist John, both members of the church music group, played guitar and sang songs for us. I tried to accompany on harmonica but it sounded like a choking swan. You see, I don't play harmonica. Dietician Heidi watched the movie with us and commented, "The only thing they have eaten in that school cafeteria is hot dogs and tater tots." Sweet! (That's my comment, not hers.)

Recreation is so valuable because it is too easy to get caught in the routine of wake, work, eat, sleep, and every few days or so, shower. Most of the troops exercise in one way or another. There are three gyms; Air Force gym is, of course, smaller than Army gym as Army has a larger contingent on base, and the third gym is the little secret no one knows about. It has aerobic machines and is much quieter, so I hear—I have yet to find out where it is. Some of us run, but it has been too muddy outside. I see a lot of runners at 04:00 or 05:00 before work. Crazy people! I shouldn't talk, because I'm probably the only one who runs with plates, vest and Kevlar helmet. I'm up to four miles. We have a "Run to Baghdad" sponsored by the gym. Each runner logs miles, either on the streets or inside on a treadmill. When you reach 100 miles, you earn a T-shirt. Actually, it is only about 40 miles to Baghdad, but I'll run the extra 60 if they don't make me leave the safety of the base!

Of course, the orthopedic surgeons are athletic and go biking together. I was able to get a sweet deal on a bike. Heidi's predecessor had left her a bike, which was to be the hospital dietician bike. Since Heidi doesn't ride, she turned it over to me on the condition that I return it for the next dietician. I kick up so much mud that there is more on the back of my neck than on my shoes when I ride, but it is a lot of fun. I have to keep my eyes open because Humvees take up much more of the road than a usual car, and it is extremely difficult for the driver to see out of the small side windows. Of course, I wear my armor on the bike as well, so in the words of our President, "Bring it on!" There is a lot of room to bike, but I try to avoid biking along the wire because it feels a little creepy with only some razor wire between me and the people who shoot mortars. In contrast to these hidden dangers, I often see only harmless-looking cows and shepherds along the fence.

Any good stretch of time off includes a visit to the PX (Post Exchange) for some shopping! The PX is well stocked, but by now I have twice looked over every piece of merchandise in there and only go to pass the time. There is a huge selection of DVDs and music CDs. Lots of local souvenirs are sold there, like wooden camels and Persian rugs, but most are overpriced and of dubious workmanship. Interestingly, there are Cuban cigars for sale. There is an alteration shop where the tailors made us some amazing scrub caps with our unit symbol embroidered on the front. Half a year ago, the PX was the site of a mortar attack. There are still the signs of the damage done by the shrapnel. One overhead lighting pole is tilted at 45 degrees, and another has a hole clean through it. There are small memorials written on the poles and on the bunkers by the bus stop. I'm relieved the mortar attacks are so greatly reduced from before, and are so poorly aimed. It would be nice if there were some way to predict where they might land, but the shells are a random and exceedingly rare risk. We just have to do our work every day and get by the best we can, the same way we get through so many worries—on faith. I had a nice surprise waiting on line in the PX, when I looked up and saw a patriotic banner sent from children in North Haven, CT. Since that is only a few miles from my hometown, I felt like their words of encouragement were a personal message from my home.

For a great night out that almost feels like being back home, we have the Sustainer movie theater. I went for the first time two nights ago with surgeon Brett from Hawaii; Paula, who is in charge of nursing; nurse Ellen, who coordinates our care of trauma patients; and nurse Marty, from the ER. It was Brett's birthday so we raised a glass in his honor. I had the Bitburg near-beer, which isn't as good as the Beck's near-beer. I hear the St. Paulie Girl near-beer is tasty, but none of them can hold a candle to beer-beer.

We talked and shared about the people we were missing. I was surprised to find that seasoned veterans with five deployments under their belts expressed their feelings of longing for loved ones and home in the same terms I was using on my first shaky deployment. I know that being separated from the ones I love will always feel wrong. Still, in this small gathering of individuals far from our families, we propped each other up like a surrogate military family, facing a common hardship. And it's difficult to call the little stresses we face hardships, as I compare our group munching chili dogs and waiting for a movie to the horrible conditions of World War II depicted in the episode of *Band of Brothers* I saw tonight.

A Black Hawk helicopter just passed overhead on its way to the hospital, and reminded me of a sad topic we discussed as we waited in the lobby of the theater. It is a tragic event that has troubled my thoughts. Several nights ago, the Medevac team landed and rushed in an American soldier who had been injured in an explosion. The Medics were giving CPR because the patient had no vital signs. Our team immediately joined them in their efforts and discovered that the soldier was a young woman. She had been fatally injured and passed away in spite of the medics' heroic attempt. Some of the younger members of the team were very hard hit. I, too, am very upset thinking about her death, and can't help but feel I am more affected because she was a woman. It doesn't make sense. Young women aren't supposed to die in war. In the end, we will be better off when none of our troops, man or woman, is dying.

Back at the Sustainer Theater, we file into our seats for the movie. It is a decent building with a big screen, and the showing was full of troops like us. There are a few differences from a movie back home. First off, the place is full of soldiers. Before the previews, right before the lights go out, a short film from the Army Signal Corps plays and the Star Spangled Banner erupts from the speakers. Our assembly springs to its feet and stands at attention in solemn respect as scenes from Normandy, Iwo Jima, Vietnam, Kuwait, and many other battles play out on the screen. After the lights go out, it's like any other theater, complete with shouts from the peanut gallery. We watched *Blade: Trinity*, and that action-packed vampire movie was just the stuff to help us forget where we were for a couple of hours.

Most of the services I have described are run by MWR (Morale, Welfare, and Recreation) and come free of charge. MWR provides the soldier with some relief from the stress of battle, and little reminders of life back home. Two nights ago, we sent two teams from our hospital to compete in the base-wide MWR dodgeball league. My team was the Hurling Panthers. Our unit symbol has a panther, and I thought the double meaning of the word "hurling" would be an apt description of our team's upcoming performance. Anesthetist Annie dubbed her team *Nefis Gowie*, which we have been led to believe means "breathe deeply" in

Arabic. After every operation on an Iraqi, I hear Annie calling *"Nefis Gowie!"* as she leans over her wakening patient. After 30 or so times I'm starting to hear it in my sleep.

We arrived at the Army gym to stare down six other teams comprised of nineteen-year-old soldiers, some of them huge! That didn't worry us much. Size just made them bigger targets, and besides, we had all recently watched the movie *Dodgeball.* Perhaps we should have practiced a bit, too. Contractor Sylvester from MWR was very happy to see we were participating. He seeded the teams and the competition began. Boundaries were marked off on the basketball court with orange cones. Six players faced off on either side. The balls were placed center court and at the referee's whistle, we sprinted to the center, grabbed all the balls we could and started throwing. I regret to inform you that the Hurling Panthers fell in the first heat. However, *Nefis Gowie* defeated their first opponent and moved on to the semi-finals.

As the second round began, the whistle was blown and the players rushed for center court. One of the big and tall Army soldiers jumped for a ball, and as he collided with another player, his shinbone buckled and folded with a resounding crack. He hit the ground and held his leg up, with his lower leg hanging at an abnormal angle at the mid-calf. Drops of blood fell from the point where the broken bone had pierced through his skin. Before this poor guy could say "blueberry pancakes", he had five surgeons pouncing on him and splinting his leg with cardboard boxes and tape provided by Sylvester. Also, it just so happened one of the other teams was an ambulance crew. They backed their bus up to the gym entrance and pulled out a stretcher. The young soldier was transported to our hospital, where orthopedic Rick took care of his leg; he was later evacuated to Germany to have a metal rod placed across the fracture. It was a bad thought, but I couldn't stop it from entering my mind. I thought, "Lucky dog, he just got handed his ticket home!" I may want to get back to Meredith and the boys, but not that way.

The episode impressed upon me how automatic our actions are in a time of need. We instantaneously switched gears from recreation to business. That is the effect of training. Training and repetition make performance of any task nearly effortless. It reminds me of the Samurai proverb: "To know and to act, one and the same". There was the same immediate delivery of effort in the care of the dying woman soldier. Starting to action is automatic, but the transition from activity to relaxation is so much harder. Our minds have difficulty handling times when there is nothing to do, and we dwell on our defeats. In the end, we have to find some peace and let the victories carry us through the bad times. That is why recreation is so precious. It's good to temporarily let go and be distracted from the real reason we are here.

I know this is long, but it all seems to flow out once I start telling it. I understand what is happening here better when I've written it out. I think it will be a long time before I know how I have changed. If you have stayed with me this long, I thank you for your interest. Be well and cherish the ones you love.

Recreationally submitted,

Chris

8

"Deep Down Inside, He Always Wanted to Be a Truck Driver."

The base of the Sunni Triangle
Saturday, 19 FEB 2005

Dear Friends,

In spite of the dictum to never start with an apology, I'll have to ask you to excuse me for not writing for so long. It's not that we have been so busy, or that I have nothing to say (fat chance of that!), but I've been in a bit of a funk lately. Could be that the Balad dust is building up inside me, or that I haven't been sleeping well, but the truth is, I just miss my family! Fortunately, Meredith and I have been able to talk frequently. And when you care for injured soldiers, you don't have to look far or long to see how fortunate you are.

This letter is really designed for my boys, and anyone else who gets a kick out of big machines. The military moves a lot of people and equipment around, and it takes a lot of powerful vehicles to get that done. This base is a beehive of mechanical activity, and without revealing anything too specific, I thought you might be interested in hearing about some of the cool stuff we drive around, or in my case, make sure doesn't run me over.

But first, let me tell you about some of the things that have been happening around Camp Anaconda. I just got back from watching part of the movie *Closer*. I'm sure it has an audience somewhere, but not a bunch of hepped-up 19-year-olds with M-16 rifles. I think the long, pained dialogue scenes, as well as the drawn out promise of physical activity, were not what we had in mind. Combine this with the fact that the audio track kept dropping out and the projectionist wasn't too quick with the reel change, and the audience began to rebel. There were catcalls, people shouting out their own lines, and best of all, soldiers waving their rifles at the screen to highlight certain features on the characters with their targeting lasers. Frankly, any movie without explosions has a challenge keeping our attention. So I left early, biked home, and figured I'd say hi to you before dropping off to sleep. I look around my hooch as I listen to the Rolling Stones and type and I find it hard to believe I am in Iraq. But soon enough, a helicopter passes overhead and I believe it.

Earlier this week, I participated in patriot detail. For those who don't recognize what that is by the name, I will explain. Our young fallen heroes depart Iraq on their somber journey home from Balad. Before they do, we gather on the runway to pay proper honor to their remains. Due to certain logistical advantages, most flights leave at night. An announcement calling for volunteers for patriot detail goes out to the base via email, and troops who are available and willing report to the airlift terminal at the prescribed time. On an earlier night, we received a distraught platoon leader with hypothermia who was extremely agitated. The second Humvee in his column had tipped off the bank of a canal in heavy rains and overturned. He had halted and quickly gone to their aid while the call was put out for rescue assistance. Fire rescue and helicopter-deployed PJ's (Para-Jumpers) plunged into the cold water. One rescuer was swept away to his death, while the others retrieved the soldiers from the submerged vehicle. Unfortunately, they had been under the cold water too long and had perished. The platoon leader was treated for his minor injuries, but our hospital chaplain did more to ease his anguish then we could do with bandages. He felt horrible, as you can imagine; we all did. It may have been little consolation to him, but his quick action kept the other soldiers in his platoon's Humvee column from also toppling into the canal. By calling for help quickly, he got everyone out of there fast and prevented them from becoming vulnerable targets. It is difficult to fathom the depth of the commitment and bravery of the rescue crews responding to the call without concern for personal safety, even to the point of making the ultimate sacrifice.

I reported to the terminal at 23:00 and queued up with the other troops, about 60 in all. There were combat troops and office clerks, ranging in rank from airman to colonel. The air was cold, and a cruel wind blew across the runway. After a few minutes, the Chief came out and explained how we would proceed. We lined up in two files and "taller tapped". This is when we look at the person in front of us and if we are taller, we tap them on the shoulder and step forward in line. When all was done, we were two columns of 30 troops, neatly arranged from tallest to shortest. As we waited, two F-16 fighter jets took off, afterburners roaring with an orange and blue cone of flame stretching out behind their engines as they were thrown skyward. The taxi lane of the runway was lined with every rescue vehicle and fireman on the base, as they wanted to bid farewell to their fallen colleague.

The C-130 cargo plane which was to carry the soldiers home landed and lowered the ramp at its tail, casting a semicircle of light from the hold onto the runway. After the 80 firefighters had formed two columns to the left of the ramp, we marched out in silence to flank the right. In front of us, a group of soldiers in full battle rattle lined up in formation. All in all, there was a cordon of about 150 troops at attention behind the plane. The ambulances from mortuary affairs pulled onto the runway, and one by one the flag-draped containers were carried past our ranks into the cargo hold by a detail of six soldiers, while we saluted each at a three-second tempo. I was cold. It was 32 degrees, and a wind at my back was chilling my bare scalp and making me shiver. I thought of the families of these four brave young men and tried to hold the most respectful salute I could muster. I tried to give these heroes a salute worthy of their service and sacrifice. It is so hard, even as I write this four days later, to contain the emotions that rush forth. The emails calling for patriot detail volunteers come often. I will march onto the runway again.

Lately, we have seen a pace at the hospital which is slower (touch wood for luck), but we aren't in the clear yet. It seems that every day at 17:00 we are sure to get the victim of an ambush or an improvised explosive device (IED) detonation. Yesterday I was the backup surgeon and my wingman, surgeon Mike, called me in at 18:30 for what the trauma coordinator said was "a sick one". In Balad, some of our soldiers had come across three insurgents arming an IED. When they engaged them, the insurgents panicked and mistakenly detonated the explosive. One perished in the blast and another was seriously injured in his chest, belly, arms, and legs. The American soldiers on the scene quickly gave emergency care to the insurgent and called in medevac. He was delivered to our hospital and Mike rushed him to the operating room. I joined in, and at one point we had four surgeons and two physicians' assistants frantically working to save this man's life. Volunteers donated blood in an emergency drive. However, he had bled too much, and even though he might have survived each of his injuries alone, the combination was too much. Perhaps he deserved what he got; we do reap what we sow, but that doesn't change that fact that it felt terrible to lose a life when the man arrived at our hospital still alive.

I pray for peace, but the war isn't quite over. We do occasionally get alarm reds after a mortar attack. One alarm this week was called for an explosion that occurred across the Tigris River in Balad. Standing on the surgeons' call building, we could see the plume of smoke rising over the palm trees to the east. We aren't the only targets in town. The insurgents are attacking Americans and Iraqis alike outside the wire.

So if I haven't depressed you completely, on to the topic I really wanted to address: how we get around. Not that we need to; I think I could live, eat, sleep, and work in the hospital for the entire four months. It is a very common sight to see one of the surgeons sleeping on the couch outside the pharmacy. Those who choose to sleep there are easy targets for a candid photograph. It is a sad fact that you can't take a nice little catnap without some yahoo disturbing your peace by whipping out a camera!

Finally, on to the heart of the matter! There are lots of ways to get around, but most commonly you will find yourself in a Humvee, or more accurately the HMMWV (High Mobility Multipurpose Wheeled Vehicle). It's a lot easier to say Humvee or Hummer. It is the workhorse of the military and ubiquitous on base. It comes in many different varieties, from an open runabout without doors to a surface ambulance with vaulted cargo ceiling and litter stands for patients. In spite of their large size, they are cramped inside. Between the passenger and driver there is a large radio console, and it would be difficult to crawl from one side to another. Many have turrets that open on top, where a gunner sits in a little sling and can rotate himself around.

Remember the fuss about armor on Humvees? Many of the early ones had cloth or thin metal doors and were vulnerable in cities or on convoy to the impact of IEDs. An unexpected risk is the fact that an IED explosion under the Humvee will injure the soldiers' legs and groin from below, and underside armor is just as important. Earlier in the war, Humvee operators would go to junkyards or steel-works and use plasma cutters to fashion thick metal panels, attach hinges, and mount them on the Humvee. Newer shipments are up-armored at the factory and have full underbody armor and tiny layered glass windows, as if the visibility wasn't challenging enough. It's easy to tell them apart because the aftermarket jobs have thick rusted doors with open air windows. The irregular cut edges are often cushioned with layers of duct tape, the soldier's best friend for any job. Which would you rather ride in? The ventilation is better in the junkyard door model, but I could wait until I was home for a breeze. Most Humvees here have a frame with fans and tubing mounted just behind the roof the cab. It is the external unit for the air conditioner, just like the fan and pump outside a home with central air.

High security Humvees outfitted for convoys have all sorts of additional armament. I don't wish to discuss these countermeasures in any detail that would betray them. Perhaps most important is the shielded gun turret on the top, which usually boasts a 50-caliber automatic weapon. Many of the Humvees that operate outside the wire carry warnings in Arabic and English on the back to protect civilian drivers from harm. These signs advise following drivers to stay back 50 meters and that lethal force is authorized. As you might guess, the soldiers must be prepared to use deadly force to protect the members of their convoy. The Humvees have to rapidly negotiate a dangerous landscape and constantly be on alert for IEDs, including vehicle borne improvised explosive devices. I have heard many stories of soldiers showing amazing restraint in holding back force when civilian drivers have drawn too close, or have driven in patterns that could have been interpreted as threatening. There are some really good guys up there in the turrets manning the 50s.

The next vehicle to tell you about is the "deuce and a half", or heavy duty truck. The two and one half refers to the tonnage it can carry. It looks like a large-cab flatbed truck you might see transporting lumber back home. They also come in many varieties, and can even carry a small crane behind the cab to load and unload cargo. Just like the Humvee found its way onto American streets as a civilian passenger vehicle, there is a street-legal version of the deuce called the "bad boy truck", which is a $300,000 extravagance marketed as a luxury overland hunting vehicle. There are many up-armored heavy trucks used for explosives recovery as well as fire and rescue work. They look like overgrown Humvees, or the real-life size equivalent of the coolest LEGO vehicles you have ever made.

Our vehicle of choice is a muddy Nissan Pathfinder. For dinner, we all cram in so we don't have to walk to the DFAC (dining facility). I often end up in the hatchback all scrunched up because I fold well. It's cool with me as long as they remember to let me out when we get there! Sometimes you have to make use of whatever equipment is present. The night we arrived, our group "commandeered" a stray van to move our gear. A surgeon always knows to make the best of available equipment. To get through the muddy, gravelly surfaces of a never-quite-finished base, a six-wheeled all-terrain buggy called a Ranger comes in handy. It looks like a golf cart that grew a mean suspension and two extra wheels. With all that mud and muck, the car wash comes in handy. The car wash is a power-stripper water jet in a corner of the hospital lot. Whenever it rains, it only takes a half-mile drive to completely cover your vehicle with thick Balad mud. You learn fast in the military the concept of RHIP (Rank Has Its Privileges). I saw our Colonel in the parking lot by his vehicle and headed over to say hi. When I saw him get in and head for the car wash, I made an about face and headed the other way before he could enlist my help.

We often see Bradley troop transport vehicles leaving the base for missions in parts unknown. It is like a compact tank with tracks on each side. It has a turret-mounted primary weapon and opens in the back for troops to enter or exit. There have been some tragedies in Iraq when these have fallen into canals, injuring or trapping the troops inside. When it is upside down, it is nearly impossible to get out. The powerhouse tank is the Abrams. It goes really, really fast on treads and can blow holes in just about anything. I often see them heading out at sunset, mounted on goose-neck trailers with the turret gunner poking his head out to catch a breeze and the last few rays of sunshine.

And now, I've saved the best for last. To an Air Force man, the aircraft are the best vehicles. Global reach and global power are achieved through air superiority. However, this will be handled by airmen other than me, as I can get quite airsick.

Ironic? After only a month, it has become easy to tell which kind of helicopter is landing just by the sound. A medevac flight departure or arrival is called "dust-off", named for the cloud of dust thrown up by the helicopter. The most frequent visitor is the Black Hawk. It moves fast, is easily maneuverable, and can carry a small number of patients in litters or on seats. At the scene, the sickest patient is loaded last, and upon arrival at our hospital, unloaded first. The helicopter blades beat a fast rhythmic pattern in midtones, like a really loud lawnmower. It approaches quickly, sometimes landing in complete darkness with the pilots using instruments and night vision goggles to reduce vulnerability from light signature.

The Chinook is an enormous double rotor helicopter which can carry many troops or patients. We are only supposed to have room for two of these on our heliport, but I have seen skillful pilots squeeze four in, the tips of their rotors practically overlapping. When they fly overhead, the air reverberates with a slow heavy "chop-chop" in deeper tones that shake the tent and seem to move the furniture back and forth a bit. The Chinooks do not have the defenses of the Black Hawk, so they are sometimes escorted by Super Cobras, attack helicopters that do not carry patients. They look and move like dragonflies; passing over head, they have a narrow silhouette, bristling with missiles and guns. Their rotor gives a high-pitched angry whine, like an amplified nest of yellow jackets. The pilots sit one behind the other.

The coolest plane on our base I've already mentioned. It is the F-16 Fighting Falcon. We routinely hear them take off at night and in the early morning. Their jets scream and rip the air over the base, and conversation has to stop until they have passed. The pilots take off with afterburners flaming and full throttle to rapidly gain altitude and safety. To watch the speed at which they flee the earth is impressive. They hustle off as if God were tossing them like a dart, or as the pilots describe it, like a homesick angel.

Well, I could go on much longer, but I've probably overstayed my welcome already! I must try to write more often, because there is so much to see and so much to say, if I wait too long the letter will be endless. There is much activity here, but as I've expressed, some sadness too. I will anxiously await a day when things are safer here and our presence is happily no longer needed by our new neighbor. Until I shuffle home, I will do my best to keep a balance of optimism and enthusiasm to provide the best care to anyone who comes through the tent flaps of our E.R., while maintaining the strength to persevere through the losses that weigh on my heart so heavily. Until we speak again, stay well, have fun, and hug the one you love.

As the sun sets behind me over Balad, I bid you good night and Godspeed,

Chris

9

"About the Bathrooms…"

A pungent corner of Mesopotamia
Monday, 28 FEB 2005

Dear Friends,

Hi, how are you? Things are going well here. I have been forced to postpone this letter for the past three days because it has been busy. And even though it is 04:00 and I have just gotten home from the hospital, I think it is best that I plug on through and get it written. First of all, if I sleep for two hours, I'm not going to feel like I got any useful sleep. Second, since I was post-call today I was able to sneak out after morning rounds and sleep a bit during the daylight hours, which was a bit of a shame because I heard it was gorgeous weather outside. And last, as I always used to say during my pre-80-hours-a-week residency, "there will be plenty of time to sleep when I'm dead!" I don't want to put off an update because last time I took too long, my friend Masey emailed me to say, "We worry about you when we don't hear from you!" I don't want you to worry about me. Honestly, I think reading what I write can't be too fun, and these newsletters probably do me a lot more good than they do you because they allow me to settle my thoughts and feelings about all the things that happen here. So here I am in the wee hours, snuggled under the blanket Meredith made me, and listening to ABBA's *Super Trouper* on my headphones. I'm trying not to make too much noise with my blanket picnic of Slim Jims, Pepsi, and some potato sticks from an MRE because the walls are paper thin and I'm not sure if my trailer mate is on the night or day shift this week.

I was called into the hospital at midnight tonight to care for two sisters, M. and S. Their father is an Iraqi soldier, and sometime earlier tonight, an insurgent threw an incendiary bomb into their house and set it on fire. M., who is two-years-old, suffered third degree burns on the entire lower half of her body and her back. S. is two-months-old, and was burned on the left side of her face and scalp. Their mother was also burned on her face and hands. Their father gathered them up and took them to first one than another hospital in town, both of which informed him that their injuries were too severe to be cared for in their facilities. In desperation, he brought them to a military unit who arranged for them to enter our base and report to our hospital.

Sometimes caring for children can make even the most seasoned nurse or doctor a bit nervous. But tonight I found every member of the team was trying to pitch in and help take care of these girls. My two partners on call tonight, surgeon Todd and surgeon Brian, told me they would be able to take care of the girls themselves if I hadn't recovered yet from being post-call, but fortunately my long nap had refreshed me. People were scrambling to find rarely used equipment for such small patients and were helping to dilute the pain medications we were using down to a safe concentration for their small bodies. We couldn't start an IV on S., so I had to do a small operation just to cut through the skin of her leg to find a vein and insert a catheter. While I worked, others patiently held her steady and shined pocket flashlights into the small incision.

With the help of the nurses and the nurse anesthetists, Todd, Brian and I cleaned their wounds and applied antibiotics and dressings to ease the pain and assist their healing. As our translator H. helped me explain to their parents, even though it would take some time in the hospital, and there would be scars, the girls have a chance to recover fully. Their serious-faced father shook my hand with his own mildly burned one and thanked me in English. I hope and pray I can get them through this.

So the past few days have been busy. The Army Combat Support Hospital (CSH or Cash) at Ibn Sina Hospital in Baghdad received so many casualties from car bombs and IEDs that some had to be transferred to our hospital. One group was in a vehicle that ran over a pile of rocks concealing explosives. The injured driver quickly got out of the vehicle and returned to help his troops on the passenger side and in the gun turret escape to safety. They were treated for burns, but they could have died if the driver hadn't rescued them. Another group was attacked by an insurgent who flung a satchel full of explosives into their Humvee. The explosions scatter fragments of metal from the bomb and the vehicle everywhere. The helmet and Kevlar vest help greatly to keep the troops alive. We removed the chest armor plate from one soldier's Kevlar vest and found a cherry-sized fragment of metal embedded halfway through its thickness. Without the armor, that fragment would have torn through his chest. In fact, with the use of armor and helmet, most of the injuries we see are in the extremities and face. For the face, the impact-resistant goggles can make a difference in saving eyesight. The past three days have seemed like an endless succession of washing extremity wounds and removing fragments from soldiers' bodies. One patient with broken legs actually had fragments of another person's bone embedded in his wounds. It could have been from a suicide bomber or from one of patient's buddies. It is such senseless violence!

It is hard to see it day after day, but we feel fortunate we can do something for these injured soldiers. We do our best to patch them up and send them on to Germany. We try to support each other and make the best of time off (when I'm not sleeping all day that is!). Neurosurgeon Lee celebrated his birthday here last week, so John from physical therapy organized a surprise party at the PX. Since we don't have anywhere else to go, it was quite well attended. After all, we are each other's surrogate family here, so we have to mark important events with the proper ceremony.

I am pleased to report that our first-string dodge ball team beat out eight teams of strapping young Army men and women to take the tournament. Go *Nefis Gowie*! My team, the Hurling Panthers, made it to the semi-finals. Fortunately there were no broken bones this week, but the heats had to be put on hold for an hour while we donned our armor and sat along the sandbagged walls in the dark during an alarm red. Our two Air Force Theater Hospital teams have yet to face each other, so we may have to schedule a grudge match.

In the spirit of *Napoleon Dynamite*, I used sandbags, plywood, a pallet, and broken chunks of wall to construct a bike jump. As you might have guessed, this was before business picked up on Thursday. I was getting some sweet air! In all truthfulness, I was not trying to get the plaster ticket home. I wore full battle rattle to defend against injury while I was jumping. But then again, I always do. It does make for a rather high center of gravity on a bike, but I'm getting used to it. Two weeks ago, I took a spill on some loose gravel, which in itself wasn't too bad, but the true casualty was my pride as this occurred in front of a crowd of logistics personnel. They were kind enough to applaud and give me generous marks for style. My fun with the jump didn't last for long, because yesterday I went behind the hospital to find it had been mysteriously dismantled. I guess the fun patrol caught wind of it. That's okay, now I'm going to start working on a half pipe.

Many remnants of the previous tenants of this base remain. There were several Mig fighter jets that Saddam kept here. These were all destroyed or damaged in the first Gulf War or Operation Iraqi Freedom. The large metal chunks that remain were lined up at one end of the junkyard. The effect is a lot like Cadillac Ranch in Odessa, Texas.

Many of you have asked, "Where do you go to the bathroom?", and I'm sure the rest of you really don't want to think about it! After being asked this question repeatedly and not really having a short answer or a civil one, I decided to tackle the subject scientifically and to settle your burning curiosity as politely as possible.

There are many inconveniences during deployment. None really compare to the difficulty of being separated from loved ones, but not having the comfort and security of your usual throne comes close. Consider that this base houses thousands of airmen, and approximately five times as many soldiers. The problem of handling our collective waste is a weighty one. The military, of course, attacks the problem with regulations. There are strict rules about where you can do your business and what you must wear on the way there. I'm sure the restrictions against unloading indiscriminately stem from historical examples of disease decimating armies far more effectively than enemy combatants. The desire to maintain a fresh-smelling base doesn't seem to be an overriding goal, as evidenced by the charming practice of continually burning garbage upwind of the hospital.

The simplest military toilets are a steel bucket covered by a piece of plywood with a hole cut in the middle. We shall refer to these as Marine toilets, and I haven't yet had the pleasure of using one, which suits me fine. When the bucket fills, whoever has displeased the sergeant that week pours kerosene in the bucket, ignites it, and stirs the contents to keep them burning until the waste is reduced to tar. The next level of technology is the portolet. Someone last week didn't know what I was talking about when I said portolet, and I realized that like "water bubbler" or "soda pop", there are regional variations in terminology. So if portolet isn't clear, other choices are port-a-john, port-a-pot, port-a-pottie, and for the Australians, port-a-loo. Beside each portolet is a hand washing station with a foot-pumped water spigot that may even have some water in it if you are having a lucky day. As expected, many visitors to the portolet feel the urgings of their muse and pen a few lines on the walls. Some of the best poetry I have read on base was found in these small spaces. The portolets at the hospital have been decorated with the red cross and crescent, but I don't know if this means that medical care is available inside. I suppose when I'm in there you could call it a doc-in-a-box operation.

If all were right in the world, one could enjoy a health break without the outside world intruding. Unfortunately, the enemy has no respect for a good morning constitutional, and the rocket which was a near miss outside the hospital a few days ago landed 15 feet from the hospital portolets. The unexploded ordnance team had to gingerly creep up, identify the unexploded rocket, and dispose of it. So I have grown particularly attached to a portolet near our hooches which is surrounded by sandbags on three sides. I think it is a great idea to have a reinforced portolet so I can continue my business through an alarm red.

The next step up in convenience, the Cadillac of toilets, is actually called the "Cadillac". These are trailers equipped with running water and showers, strategically placed on the opposite side of housing from my hooch, so they are as far a walk as possible. This makes going to the Cadillacs a real expedition. I pack my toiletries, change of clothes, and towel, then don armor and I'm off on the journey! One can't forget a bottle of drinking water because the water in the Cadillacs is not safe to drink. At the door, we check the sign to see if combat showers are in effect. Combat showers are not some kind of "don't ask, don't tell" drill; they are simply water rationing rules if water supplies are low. You jump in, turn on the water when you are under the spigot, and use 30 seconds to wet down. Next, turn off the water, and soap and shampoo until you are satisfied. Finally, turn on the water again, use 60 seconds to rinse, and your shower is done! Anyone who has ever shared a bathroom with me knows I don't even get started during the first 90 seconds of my half-hour shower. I have decided to compensate by not showering for a while and later taking several combat showers in a row!

The top brass (O-5's and above) rate a wet trailer of their own and share a toilet and shower with only one other person. Our little cadre is fortunate in that surgeon Todd has let us drop buy to use the facilities in his hooch, F-22, whether it be Fashion TV on the satellite broadcast or a hot shower. F-22 has become the nerve center for the surgical service.

The flow of water in and out of the base is an incredibly complex affair which I only partially understand. There is one truck that brings in potable water, which isn't really potable. However, this water is used to fill the tanks outside the Cadillacs. Water that comes out of the shower drains is called "grey water", and water that comes out of the portolets and toilets is called "black water". There are different trucks for handling each. A crew has the unenviable job of evacuating the portolets into black water trucks. The next part is even stranger. Late at night, those black water trucks hook up with different black water trucks and the contents are pumped from one to the other. This second group of trucks is used to truck the water off the base to another location. Where, I do not know. These trucks that go off the base are decorated with a rainbow of colored lights on both sides. On first thought, you might ponder why a truck taking the dangerous convoy route would call attention to itself with colored lights. The best I can figure is that the lights are warning, "Don't blow me up, or else you'll be wearing it!"

Well, that's all I've got to say about that, as Forrest Gump would say. I can't believe I am sending friends a document full of descriptions of toilets. Hopefully, it answers all the questions you asked and others you were too polite to ask.

It's almost 07:00 and I have to change to get back to work. I have to perform a skin graft on an Iraqi policeman upon whom I operated the first night I was on call. It is a big step forward that he has healed enough from his wounds to have them covered with a skin graft. It is very rewarding to me to know every day he is getting stronger; yesterday, I even saw him sitting outdoors in the sun. Have a good time, all the time!

Your brother in arms,

Chris

10

"Meet the Iraqis"

Mortaritaville, Iraq
Sunday, 6 MAR 2005

Dear Friends,

I hope this letter finds you all in good health and happy in the warmth of your families. Today is a hazy, cool, breezy day in Balad. It is probably 60 degrees outside, but in the sun it feels okay. I am once again chillin' in the hooch, and taking advantage of a slow afternoon to catch up on correspondence. I have Duran Duran playing on Armed Forces Network Radio, the military station "broadcasting from an undisclosed location in Iraq" and boasting "the most heavily armed staff on the airways." After performing burn wound care on my two young patients, I have had absolutely nothing to do today. Since I actually slept last night, something I have a lot of trouble doing, I am skipping the Sunday afternoon nap.

Things have been calm here lately. Last night, I helped surgeon Todd take care of an Iraqi National Guard recruit who was struck with small arms fire. We reexplored his abdomen and repaired an injured artery in his left leg. That is Todd's specialty, and he was kind enough to teach me some of his techniques as we rebuilt the man's artery using one of his own veins, sewing a tiny watertight seam between the two vessels. With luck, that will last his whole life and most importantly, he will not lose his leg. He looked to be about 40, which is not an uncommon age for new soldiers in Iraq. I've mentioned before how I am so inspired by their bravery to join up. I also think for many it is the only industry hiring at this time.

Much of my time recently has been occupied by being the combat pediatric surgeon, and even pediatrician. I think the word is out on the street to bring children to my base. A few nights ago, the guards at the gate called to say that a couple and their two children were requesting to be admitted to have their 4-year-old boy's burned leg looked at. They had visited the hospital downtown in Balad, and had been told, "Go see the Americans!" So not only are we doing it like they do downtown, we are doing it better. In addition, the parents wanted me to check out their other son who had something wrong with his reproductive organs. Why not? Let them in, I communicated to the guards.

The family showed up. The father was ebullient, shaking everyone's hand and thanking us not only for letting them in, but also thanking us for each and every service member in Iraq fighting for his country's freedom. His four-year-old boy, a worried little man with a tiny burn on his thigh, was quickly treated and dressed by my colleague, surgeon Mike. His inconsequential burn from some spilled coffee would have gotten better even if ignored. The boy's pregnant mother smiled and thanked us warmly as we handed him back to her.

Now the 18-month-old younger boy was a different matter. He was none too happy to meet me and eyed me with suspicion and anger most of the time I was near him. I examined him in front of his parents and found that he had a condition known as intersex anomaly. He was so worked up with us that it took a sedative for him to get his x-rays. Intersex anomaly is when a person's body forms some male parts and some female parts. Even though I have picked up a little Arabic, perhaps enough to order a beer in a restaurant (if there was a beer to be had), I knew I needed some extra help. I called for translator M., who was on duty for the evening, and sat down with the boy's parents.

I have had this discussion with parents before, and even when all parties speak the same language, it is difficult. Here I was, a stranger from a different country, speaking a different language, telling them their cute little boy was internally a girl and had a womb. For every statement I made, first the translator had to get over his shock, and then when he told the parents, they had to get over their shock.

I don't have all the tests to care for this boy at my disposal, here in our tent hospital, but what we found on examination and ultrasonography was fairly clear. Had I met this youngster when he was born, I would have advised his parents to raise him as a female, because the adjustment and growth would be easier for the child. The situation made me consider that this recommendation takes into account the culture and the medical resources available in the United States. How would this decision be different in Iraq? After speaking for some time and letting the facts sink in, I told them I still thought the child would have an easier life if raised as a female. No, no, and definitely no was the father's response. Imagine how any of you might feel in his position! As long the boy was alive and his parents could raise him, that was enough for them. They accepted he would not be able to have children of his own. I told them there was no emergency and their boy could live a full and happy life. He will require hormone therapy and surgery when he becomes an older child. I spelled out all my recommendations in a letter they can carry with his medical records and a copy of his CT (computed tomography) scan on a compact disc. I told them, no one, not friends or family, needs to know this private part of their boy's life, only that they had to make sure their boy understood his condition as he grew older. The father seemed somewhat comforted by this, and all in all, the family just seemed relieved their children were in no danger.

The father thanked everyone he could lay his hands on in the hospital. He was formerly a mechanic, until Saddam dissolved his company, and had been getting by on piecework since then. I learned a new idiom from him. He said when he brought his children to the an Iraqi hospital, they turned him away, and treated him like "Ali Baba". Apparently, Iraqis don't have a high opinion of Ali Baba of the "40 thieves" fame. If you treat a person like "Ali Baba", you are "dissing" him. Recently, it has become a term used by Iraqis to refer to insurgents. The family stayed with us overnight because the gates had been secured for the evening. In the morning, they departed, in search of an endocrinologist at Medical City in Baghdad. I called Iraqi Dr. O. at Balad Hospital to try to help locate one.

Iraqi Dr. O. is our liaison with Balad Hospital. Dr. O. is our friend! Dr. O. helps us find homes for the Iraqi patients who are better but not strong enough to return to duty or be independent. Once or twice a week, he visits our hospital and makes rounds with chief of staff George, who coordinates transfers to Iraqi hospitals. I helped pick up Dr. O. at the north gate once. I had to check out a weapon, as we need to have a loaded weapon when approaching the gate. Of course I took out an M-16. At the gate, we waited for Dr. O. to get searched and wanded for weapons, and then we served as escorts to bring him back to the hospital. Dr. O. has had an interesting training. He has done a year here, a year there, and even one year of general surgery. He is sort of a medical jack-of-all-trades. Two days a week he goes to Baghdad to work for a pharmaceutical company; that is, when he can get to Baghdad. In the military, we get a skewed view of distances. Nowhere in the country is more than an hour or so away by helicopter. It's different when you are on the ground, in a taxi or POV (that's Privately Owned Vehicle for you non-military types). One of our patients had to get home to Fallujah, and I asked translator A. how far that was. He said it used to be an hour, but now it is four hours, with checkpoints. And then he added the usual statement about getting anywhere in Iraq, "that is, if you can get there".

Our translators are essential to doing business. They usually hang out in their tent behind the hospital, and the loudspeaker constantly blares out cries of "interpreter to ward three". They have picked up a lot of medical knowledge and always urge the patients, "do some deep breathing", "get up and walk", or "keep that wound clean". Sometimes you will ask them to say something simple such as telling the patient to stand and walk, and a long conversation will ensue. I think they are throwing in their own opinion of the patients who are being lazy, and motivating them by comparing them to little girls if they don't get off their butts and start facilitating their own recovery.

The patients are a continual source of triumph and drama. It is so rewarding to see the men recover from their wounds and begin to act alive again after being nearly blown to smithereens. One man had burned his hands and feet in a gas fire and had learned to care for his wounds himself. Each week I would perform a painful dressing change and he never made a sound.

Upon discharge from the hospital, one patient jumped up in his underwear and demonstrated how would dance when he got back to Baghdad. When we told him he couldn't get on the helicopter without pants, he promptly began stripping the pants off the sleeping patient next to him. The nurse on the ward, who had the most vested interest in making sure this particular patient didn't miss the chopper to Baghdad, ran to find him pants. She gave him the bum's rush out of the tent onto the helipad with his drawers drooping before he could try any more stunts.

We asked another patient, an Iraqi colonel commanding the local Iraqi National Guard unit, what he would do when he was discharged from the hospital. He had undergone two operations for a gunshot wound to the abdomen. He pointed to his belly and replied in English, "I know who did this; I wish to repay him the favor." Another man who returned to clinic was not healing his wound very well. He was only eating one meal a day of rice and vegetables. I told him he would have to stay in the hospital for a week for surgery and "three hots and a cot". He replied that maybe I should keep him in for two weeks.

Outside the wire, I can often see the local farmers working the land. They tend sheep, goats, and cows, and sometimes till the fields with tractors. The children wear brightly colored robes and sometimes they even wave hi!

There are signs of Saddam's Iraq. In the fighter logistics building there are some murals dating from the previous owners of this base. They depict the Iraqi Air Force Mig jets soaring triumphantly and blazing across the sky. It is ironic that these murals are next to a display case of fragments and relics collected from the wreckage of the Migs and other equipment when the US forces first marched onto this base. When neurosurgeon Lee visited Baghdad, he found an even more interesting mural on the ceiling of one Saddam's many palaces. (Early on, UN inspectors were forbidden from entering palaces. Just about everything was designated a palace after that.) It depicts a heated battle between the Iraqi Republican Army and an invading force. The Iraqis are decimating the invaders. I think the viewer can assume the opponents are U.S. forces because of the Chinook helicopter and other recognizable equipment.

Also on our base is a mosque. It is closed up and we are forbidden from entering the grounds, as per General Order 1A, which delineates forbidden behaviors (such as drinking alcohol) to respect host nation values.

Our other contacts with Iraqis are the many who work on the base. Each day, they enter via the gate I described earlier. There is much building, moving, buying, selling, and processing done on the base. One wonders how long we are planning for this base to be here. If nothing else, it must be a great source of jobs.

I found a mini-golf course on base! It has an appropriate theme for our camp, and is called the "Balad Airbase Golf War Putting Course". The barriers and traps are modeled after items we frequently encounter when trying to get from place to place. There are fences, vehicle barriers, barbed wire, helmets, and bunkers. At least the golf balls don't explode.

I have to thank everyone who has sent me St. Patrick's Day decorations! They have been put to good use around the hospital, and do a great job cheering up the troops and letting them know that people back home are thinking of them. Not much else is going on. I'm girding up my loins for a long operation tomorrow. I will be grafting skin onto the leg burns of the two-year-old girl. It will probably be a four-hour case in a 90 degree room. I'll lose a few pounds. Don't think I'm complaining—BRING IT! There are hardships about being here, but nothing feels better than doing what I've been trained to do and being of some use to the people of this country. So it's on like *Donkey Kong*!

As the moon rises over housing area H4 and the dust drifts across our sky, I bid you farewell. I miss you very much and can't wait to get home. Until then, I'll be thinking of you and I'll keep trying to do my best. Be mellow, and love life!

Signing off until next time,

Chris

11

"This Old Hooch"

LSA Anaconda, Iraq
Thursday, 10 MAR 2005

Dear Friends,

It is a dark and stormy night. The rain pelts the corrugated metal roof of my trailer like tiny footfalls. The rain runs down the inside of my door, and then drips back out onto the steps, leaving trails of dirt like the paths of teardrops. The air is quite cool, and after my run (eight miles in armor, oh yeah!) I was soaked to the bone, splattered in mud but at a perfect temperature. I got a little nervous about the prospect of running the perimeter and turned back to internal streets when I reached the wire. I'm sure I'm in no danger from the enemy, but I saw a number of trucks slide and hydroplane onto the shoulder and the perimeter is not designed for foot traffic, nor is it permitted. With the myriad rules in the military, it is a novelty to come across one that makes plain sense. So I make my miles by zigzagging across the base, passing by housing, depots, runways, and construction sites. It is a bit like the Snake Run on College Hill in Providence, but without the hill.

In order to further share the experience of a self-proclaimed epicurean in Balad, and to show how thankful I am for the gifts of hot sauce, I want to share my meal with you. Don't worry, just the thoughts, not the actual raw matter. Although I did spill a little on the postcard I sent to Ben, so it should be ripe by the time it arrives stateside.

Tonight's treat was a MRE enjoyed indoors, in refuge from the rain. I didn't look too closely when I grabbed the MRE from the hospital DFAC and discovered too late that I had #12 Veggie Burger in BBQ Sauce. No worries, I knew I had my trusty sauce. I thought Neera's Caribbean Salsa (A Tropical Delight), generously provided by friends Gary and Joanne, would be the perfect antidote. The MRE was well-stocked, with the aforementioned burger, sliced dried cranberries, two packages of freeze-dried wheat bread, the condiment package (including iced tea mix), Charms fruit candy, and a chocolate chip brownie. The burger was warmed with the heater, which I activated with some lime Koolade, adding a scent of citrus and hydrogen gas to the atmosphere. Aside from the disturbing consistency of the patty (textured protein concentrate of soy protein isolate), the pineapple and honey of the salsa with jabs of red chile and habenero made for a delightful meal!

I mentioned earlier that I was caring for a two-year-old girl with leg burns. Today I took her to the operating room to have a look at her skin grafts. I was nervous about her prospects because I had placed the grafts three days ago at a frenzied pace. Our hospital suddenly received 14 injured Iraqis, interrupting my operation. There had been two suicide car bombs, one in Baqoubah and another around the corner in Balad city. The bomb in Balad detonated at a police station which happened to be next door to a school. Today I spent part of the afternoon with Dr. O. from downtown. He filled me in on his hospital's experience last Monday. They received many children with minor injuries and three who were declared dead on arrival. He expressed his hope that such events would someday occur less frequently. I replied that I hoped soon they wouldn't happen at all, and couldn't help but add, "That's why we are here." As we looked at each other, two doctors cleaning up after careless misguided men, I think we both realized the situation was more complex than that. Once again I felt lucky to be a doctor, where the goals are more simple and pure. I appreciated solidarity with Dr. O. in the war against pain and lost limbs and life. We continued in the business of locating supplies in critical demand at his hospital and identifying patients who were ready for transfer to his care, under the direction of chief of staff George, who has the grueling and often thankless job of liaison to Iraqi medical services.

So three days ago, as I was laying down an artisan skin graft at a luxurious pace, the choppers started landing. The room was needed, and fast. I had already harvested thin shavings of skin from M.'s thighs and I could not bring myself to abandon the operation and throw them away. With the skillful help of tech Twila, who came to my rescue with her burn treatment experience, we stapled the skin graft to M's legs at a furious pace and got her out of the operating room to make way for the critically injured patients.

Everyone put on their game face and the hospital went into high gear. Surgeon Brett, physician assistant Steve, and I worked on a policeman who was bleeding from an artery in his shoulder and another artery in his chest. As we called out for equipment and supplies, the OR crew worked with us as if we were parts of the same machine. In the same operating room, orthopedic Rick worked on a man whose arms and legs had been riddled with shrapnel. All the other surgeons were participating in similar scenes in the other two operating rooms, and it continued until late into the night. Of the two children we received from the school in Balad, both teenagers, one had a head injury and the other had an arterial injury that required surgeons Brian, Todd, and Jay's efforts for hour after hour to save his arm. Working here in Iraq, one of the greatest sources of pride and satisfaction to me is the confidence I have in each and every one of my partners. They are solid, skillful surgeons in whose hands I would trust my own life.

So today, little M. was sedated and I gently peeled back the bulky layers of dressings and splints that made her legs look disproportionately large. The skin graft looked a little hastily cobbled at the corners, but thankfully it had the dusty rose color of newly forming blood vessels. It had taken root like a piece of sod transplanted to a bare lawn. On a daily basis, I find myself in awe of the miracle of the body's capability for recovery even in the face of our rough and clumsy meddling. It reminds me of Ambrose Pare's frequent statement in his records of injured French soldiers: "I dressed the wound, God healed it." M. has come a long way since the day her house was burned down, and she still has a long way to go. With a little luck and all the fine care she is receiving from our skilled intensive care nurses, she may just survive.

On the evening after the mass casualty, we had the bittersweet occasion to bid farewell to one cadre of Aussies and happily welcome another. The group of Australian doctors and nurses had been keeping the hospital running before our group showed up in January, and were faithful partners to us and the Air Force group before us. The pagoda by the morale tent in the hospital lot was stocked with sodas, near-beer, chips, and cake. A CD with a mix of music prepared by the Australian ICU doctor, who like me takes care of babies when not in a war zone, played Men at Work and the Brothers Gibb on a portable stereo. Our commander, surgeon Chuck, presided over the presentation of certificates of admiration and appreciation to the able Aussies. ER tech Heather, who can swing her hair like Wayne and Garth, got us all dancing to *Staying Alive*, which made me wonder if somehow real beer had been slipped into the ice tub. Just when everyone was having a good time, the insurgents, who obviously hate fun as much as they hate freedom, launched a dud shell somewhere near the base and we all had to abandon the pagoda for the cement bunker. Our spirits couldn't be damped, and we sang *Tie Me Kangaroo Down* and *Yankee Doodle* until the "all clear" sounded and we could come out. The full day of operating had left me drained, so I stumbled home after that to crash.

I have been blessed recently with the kindness of so many thoughtful people back home. A youth group from Wallingford, CT sent such encouraging and patriotic letters. I received packages from the Knights of Columbus in Totowa, NJ with niceties for the soldiers and treats for the children. The Johns Hopkins Medicine alumni office put together a riotous package with great decorations and school paraphernalia. And generous friends have sent me letters and delicious snacks for us to share. I was so happy, too, that Paulie and Erin visited Meredith and our boys, and it comforts me greatly to know they had a fun visit. It means so much to us over here to know you are thinking of us and sending your support. Thank you for remembering us and keeping us in your prayers. I'm also very happy to have my *Rocky* poster in The Swamp so I can dig down and find the eye of the tiger.

It's a matter of concealment, but items in the military—buildings, clothes, vehicles—are the same boring, drab, dull earth tones. People aren't over here long before they start putting their personalized touches on things. You can see this in our homes, or rather, the trailer park. Walking through the rows, I pass by flags, stickers, and name signs. One colonel has a great pink flamingo outside of her hooch. In addition to adding a little bright color to the suburb, it lets her pick her trailer out from all the nondescript identical ones around it. I don't know who put it there, but I have also seen a pink flamingo in miniature desert camouflage uniform and helmet. Anesthetist Annie has a birdfeeder on her back window, a gift from her sister. I read a piece her sister wrote for their local paper in New Hampshire, where she described the outpouring of support from the staff at the store where she bought the feeder when they learned that it was for a deployed service member saving lives in Iraq. It was a touching story and showed me in very poignant terms how hard it must be on the folks back home who want to do anything to make our stay easier. I realize how much it means to them to be able to send us a little comfort from home.

I miss my garden. I miss deadheading the roses and looking for a stem to send into Meredith with the boys, telling them to claim it as their own. I even miss the stubborn little weeds that hide among the thorny roots and suckers. I've planted a little herb garden in the sandbags surrounding my hooch. I just cut holes in the fabric and pushed the seeds in. I have a few outside my door on the southern exposure, and some in the sandbags under my window. I even planted tomatoes in the sunniest spot, but that's just absurd. With the recent rains, I have been rewarded with a few tender sprouts of cilantro peeking out of the holes. Soon I will be able to look at plants outside my window through the more functional decoration of duct tape Xs, which are to prevent the glass from shattering if there is an impact nearby.

Traveling around base, I run into a lot of humorous recognition of our title of "Mortaritaville". The "Oasis Hotel", the dwelling place of a squadron out of Korea, has a tally of mortar hits posted at their front gate. One of the logistics tents has a mock-up of an unexploded shell halfway through its sandbags. The motor pool has spray-painted "Monster Garage" on one of their sheds in the yard, where they maintain and repair the Humvees and other military vehicles. The H6 housing area has a great *M*A*S*H*-style sign post with boards listing the distances to various home cities of the occupants. On this post, the distance to Hell is listed as 0 miles. No decoration beats the huge American flag painted on the 16 foot bunkers surrounding Town Hall.

Decoration is also applied to the vehicles. I found a truck with its name, "The Beast", stenciled on the front bumper. Or perhaps the title refers to the driver? Many of the vehicles are emblazoned with their drivers' names in tape on the windshield. Personally, I think the visibility in a Humvee is so limited I wouldn't squander a spare inch of view. However, I did appreciate the Humvee with "4-Month Bachelor" proclaimed on its windshield. Look out! If I had a Humvee, I think it would have a Tabasco sauce and razor wire hood ornament like the one I found outside the DFAC.

Even in the hospital, there's time for some fun and games. In a period of rest between cases, we clowned around with a huge mallet for pounding in tent stakes which had been left behind by the logistics folks. I always wanted to be an orthopedic surgeon! Just think, Mom, I could be hanging out in Madison making a mint! I'm just kidding! Also in our free time, we have all been busy trying to grow our moustaches. The morale committee has brought us "March Moustache

Mania". I hear next month brings "April Armpit Attack" for the ladies. Take care of the ones who bring you joy!

I remain,

Chris

12

"Along the Shore"

The Island of Balad
Monday, 14 MAR 2005

Dear Friends,

I address you as friends because it is the simplest way I can express my affection for you. Thank you for your interest, attention, and encouragement. I have heard from so many of you and it keeps me going. Living on the base is like island life. I am far from home, in a new and exciting land, but I'm trapped here. My connections with the outside world are whatever can be shipped, flown, or transmitted in. I cannot go out and get it myself. (Isn't it odd how contents moved by land are shipments and by sea are cargo?) So today, in recognition of my boundaries, I decided to explore the shore of this island.

But first, another meal! The sauce featured tonight is one that will be familiar to friends in Texas, and probably some others elsewhere. Cholula Sauce is billed as "*El sabor autentico de la salsa Mexicana*". The meal I chose to sample this "authentic flavor" was the MRE with the suspicious title "Chicken breast, chunked and formed, in salsa". The flavor of Cholula, much like the label, is earthy, yet transcendent. The label, fraught with contradictions, features a woman framed in an adobe archway. She wears an ethereal white robe, but her features are thick. She prepares a peasant meal, while her eyes gaze at things beyond us. Am I reading into it too much? I think not! The flavor inside is sublime. It is at once sweet, with the rich tanginess and scent of tomato, but stealthily followed with the measured bite of cayenne pepper in the back of the throat. The ingredients list red and piquin peppers as well as the secretive catchall "spices", but I say hidden under the milled wooden top is nothing short of gustatory intrigue!

As you can tell, we are not very busy! It is good to see the soldiers injured in the explosions on the 7th in Balad and Baqouba improving and leaving for home one by one. The helicopters still drop off the occasional injured patient, Americans residing with us briefly before moving on. Nearly every day provides another example of the toughness of our dedicated troops. One Special Forces operative stayed overnight before moving on to Germany. Injured Special Forces troops arrive and leave mysteriously, and they share the same fake last name and invented social security number for secrecy's sake. This man had suffered injuries to his eye, lung, and arm in an explosion and was on a ventilator, but was most upset that the insurgent attack had blown off part of his favorite tattoo on his bicep. Another colonel came to us with an infected gallbladder. Rather than leave the theatre and have the less painful laparoscopic surgery, he chose to stay with us and undergo surgery with the larger open incision so he could stay near his troops. Surgeon Brian removed an absolutely breathtaking gallstone from his battered gallbladder. It was about two inches across, a real keeper! The colonel toughed it out and is recovering superbly.

I am very pleased that the past few days have brought further improvement to the two burned babies in my care. As M. has gotten better, she has become more animated and interactive. This morning she was shoveling fistfuls of scrambled near-egg into her mouth, and has become a huge fan of the soft drink Sprite. Her skin grafts have taken root, and tomorrow I hope to graft the remainder of her deep burns. Although she will carry the scars for life, if her strong spirit at this point is any indication, she will overcome this hardship. Her baby sister S. is also doing wonderfully, and we often hear her lusty cries for formula throughout the hospital when she realizes it is mealtime. Her face is healing quickly; I may not even need to use a skin graft. These two sweethearts have enjoyed the stuffed animals, puddings, and other treats I have received from home, and I do appreciate what you have sent.

Not all of the days are easy. I need to tell you the sad story of a baby we could not save. In Fallujah, a pregnant mother lay in the hospital for three days, and as best as we can tell, her newborn contracted an infection during childbirth. When he suffered seizures and difficulty breathing on his first day of life, the doctors contacted our forces in the region, who mobilized a helicopter medevac crew to move this six-pound fragile patient to our hospital. Drawing on the help of the ER staff, as well as the ICU doctors and nurses, we were able to resuscitate the baby and hook him up to a breathing machine. His father rode in the helicopter with him and lived in the hospital cot next to his tiny son for the short week he was alive. He thanked me repeatedly for doing what I could for his boy. He also said what many other Iraqis have said to me; he wanted to thank each and every soldier for leaving their homes to risk their lives and help the Iraqi people.

The time came when it was clear we could not keep his fragile newborn son alive for long. Even if we did, he would likely be crippled with brain damage, seizures, and cerebral palsy. The discussion I had to have with his father is one I've had before, but every time it is just as horrible. I told him that it was better the baby die gently than have us continue to force his little body to stay alive with machines. I told him if it was my boy, I wouldn't want him to go through it anymore. It rips at my heart to even imagine it. His father told me he was so thankful we had tried, and he didn't think there was any way his son could survive. He seemed to accept it more peacefully than I could. The unlucky translator who had to transmit this conversation was visibly shaken. Then the father held his baby in his arms as he died. I hope and pray I can better help the next baby who comes our way.

As I sat in my hooch writing the paragraph above, there was a thundering boom that shook the trailer. Not to worry, it was just something called a controlled detonation. A controlled detonation is when the explosives crew blows up unexploded material, suspicious bags, or abandoned vehicles on and around the base. As it is 23:30, I wasn't expecting a controlled detonation, and I nearly had an uncontrolled detonation of my own. Before I knew what the noise was, I suited up, grabbed my gear, and headed to the hospital, in case there was a need for help. It had been detonated just over the wire from the hospital, and was even louder to the crew on duty. Bits of gravel had landed on the roof. Most of the staff and patients hit the deck when they heard the noise. Even the colonel recovering from his gallbladder operation jumped up and out of bed. He needed a little help to get off the floor when the commotion died down. I'm glad I went in, because Brian and Mike were operating on the chest of a man who had been injured and I stayed to observe.

Now that I'm back in the hooch, and it is 01:40, I'm feeling the fatigue of my tour of the shore today. When we finished work around noon, it was a gorgeous Sunday outside. I had wanted to explore the shore of our razor-wire ringed island, and it seemed like the perfect opportunity. One option would have been the base shuttle bus, piloted by a local national contractor driver. I was afraid the regimented stop, open doors, shut doors, and start of the circuit of bus stops wouldn't lend itself to the spirit of rambling I was after. So I loaded up my bicycle with repair kit and pump, strapped on armor, weapon, Camelbak water pack, and helmet and headed north. Along the perimeter there are a few things to see. Rather than risk security by describing a specific organization of the base, I'll mention a few sites in no particular order. There are Humvees, passenger vehicles, heavy trucks, and water trucks circling the base in both directions endlessly. I guess there is just a lot of stuff to be moved from here to there, and back again. I pass by lots of KBR areas: cargo storage, vehicle staging, construction sites, and worker housing. I even found the convoy staging area. I wonder if they have heard of the Rubber Ducky in Iraq.

The circumference of the base is not much, a little longer than the training ride Meredith and I used to do for the triathlon. I know that doesn't help the rest of you, but I don't want to be too specific. Of course it is harder to judge distances on a mountain bike, which I am not so used to riding. With all the truck traffic, I spent much of the ride on the shoulder, or even further off the road, in the mud and ruts. But a mountain bike is fun when you find a hill or bumps for catching sweet air.

I got to look out over the wire at lots of farm land. Many families were out following tractors, or tending livestock. Men and women were working together. Children would sometimes be pitching in, but were mostly just going about the business of being children. One was riding a donkey, slapping his rump with a twig and turning him so he walked in endless circles. Two others were singing a chant in raised voices and laughing at the end of each verse. If they were like me and my brothers, they were probably making fun of me as I rode by. The children all waved to me, as did most of the adults.

I saw a bird alight on the wire, caw, and then take off over a two story home. Most of the structures were mud huts, but these seemed to be temporary shelters for shepherds. Everywhere the ground was exploding with growth in green rows beyond the canal and the mud. Life seemed to go on, as if war was something far away which did not concern the people of Balad, and certainly didn't change the necessity of planting. It is such a gesture of hope to plant a seed. It holds inherent the belief that you will be there in the future to reap the rewards of your efforts. Along the Tigris, tall palms marked the most fertile and soaked soil. More brown houses were tucked in their shadow. Men walking home from work parted at doorways and entered for the midday meal. I even found a respectable palm tree on the base, standing out from the long row of eucalyptus trees planted along the inside of the perimeter.

I'm probably speaking prematurely, and I have to see what the local mortgage rates and school districts are like, but I think I have found a comfy vacation home near the base. All we need is a satellite dish and an above-ground pool, and it will be a little slice of heaven! So what do you think, Meredith?

Rounding the base, I found one of the many "Yugos" that mark the landscape. They are large pyramidal bunkers built by Yugoslavian crews for the previous owners. I tried to ride my bike up them, but they were a little too steep. Orthopedic Brian was able to ride them, but did leave a bit of his arm skin behind.

This brought me full circle around our little island, and back to my hooch. It reminded me that our island was recently graced and honored with the visiting luminaries known by the accurate, but creatively spelled, moniker "Purrfect Angelz". We had known for weeks they were coming. Promises of outdoor aerobics sessions and visits to the hospital were floated. As the thoughtful doctor I am, I knew that a visit from the "Angelz" would only speed my patients' recovery by harnessing the healing power of their buoyed spirits. Orthopedic Brian and I wanted everything to be "Purrfect" for their visit. After all, these were Angelz visiting us. They could have chosen sunning in Cancun or shopping in LA for spring break, but instead they decided to risk their tails hopping from base to base in Black Hawks, and performing up to three shows a day in front of muddy soldiers. So Brian and I busied ourselves polishing the shine on the hospital's apple.

But then, in came the unwelcome news that heavy weather had grounded the Angelz' helicopter, and they would not be able to visit. "What about the patients? How would they take it?" I worried. To ease my troubled mind I tramped through the mud to see a showing of *Man of the House*, hoping a light farce with Tommy Lee Jones and some University of Texas cheerleaders would distract me from my troubles. But then, the movie was cancelled, a makeshift sound system hastily assembled, and the Angelz took the stage. Around 250 Army soldiers and I cheered heartily. Here was a troupe of five friendly, talented American women who had traversed the globe to shore up the troops' spirits. Their act looked a lot like the cheerleading competitions shown on ESPN 2 or 3, except the costumes had a touch of Madonna or Daisy Duke thrown in. I ran back to the hospital and got a list of all the wounded heroes' names, and the Angelz provided autographed pictures for every one of them. Then, as quickly as they had descended on Balad, they were off to Mosul to cheer the troops there.

As you can see, life is grueling for us here, but we somehow struggle through the day. We know we are blessed to be Americans. We will keep doing our best here. God grant us the strength to fulfill our duties and the compassion to ease the burden upon those damaged in this war. I miss you and I miss home. Stay safe and have fun!

In Deo Speramus,

Chris

13

"Walk by It Once And You Own It"

Land of 1001 Arabian Nights
Saturday, 19 MAR 2005

Dear Friends,

It is late Friday night, the temperature is dropping in the plains along the Tigris, but Billie Holiday is singing *I've got my love to keep me warm*. My love is far away, but just the thought of her warms my heart, and I smile as I imagine the day we will be together again.

So much has happened, it is hard to begin. Even though I know I wrote you a few short days ago, it seems like much more time has passed. When things are busy, and we are active, the days just melt away. Still, my short little four months over here seem to be dragging along, and the finish line so far off. So now I find myself, halfway done, and the best I can do is just take the rest of it day by day.

I guess it is easiest to start with midnight snack! Tonight's treat was a beef stew MRE pouch, beef jerky, and wasabi rice crackers. The beef stew has become an old familiar experience, from the warm homey smell and hearty taste to the thick consistency with mushy potato chunks mixed in. It is definitely stick to your ribs fare, even if the meat chunks are compressed cubes diluted with unmentionable adulterants. Even this considerable goodness can be improved with just the right sauce. Since St. Pat's day has just passed, I chose Goodall's of Dublin Irish Steak Sauce. The label sported a vibrant green shamrock, albeit the common three-leaf variety, so I knew I could expect a modicum of luck. The ingredients of apples, dates, and molasses further piqued my interest. Opening the bottle released a deep tangy bouquet, and the thick sauce shimmered truculently in its glassy well. It was so thick it wouldn't budge from its home until I had broken the surface with the back of my spoon. The steak sauce was an excellent compliment to the stew, nearly transforming it into something that could be called a meal. I washed down my near-meal with a cocktail of half-purple Gatorade and half-green Gatorade, resulting in a citrus double-strength liquid with the sickly color of antifreeze but a marvelous palate.

The title above, "Walk by it once and you own it", I picked up somewhere in my Air Command Staff College course. The gist is, when you see something out of order, and you walk by it, you are condoning it and accepting it as your standard. It could be something as trivial as a ball of dirty tape in the elevator at the hospital, or as big as a gas leak. This is such a big base with so much Brownian motion that I feel like there are countless risks for error, and similarly, countless opportunities to improve conditions and possibly head off disaster.

I got home late tonight because I was operating with surgeon Brett. An American soldier was brought to our hospital with a wound. As it turned out, this wound was serious and accompanied by internal bleeding that required emergency surgery. This isn't anything out of the ordinary for a night at our hospital, but what was different is this injury occurred on base, as a result of a fellow soldier's actions. It troubles me to see a completely preventable injury with life-threatening consequences occur at the hands of a friendly force. As a result, one soldier is leaving the theater for an uncomfortable recovery and will wear a scar for life, while another soldier faces possible disciplinary action and also must carry the burden of guilt for what happened. I know I'm being vague, but there is no more of the situation I can share. It just frustrates me to see unnecessary additions to the suffering in this war. I think when you take a hundred thousand 19-year-olds, arm them to the teeth, and ship them overseas, events like this are bound to happen.

We made the most of our St. Patrick's Day in "O'raq". The day started with a ten-kilometer road race. As in most events here, 97% of those participating were Army troops. One company even had shirts made and ran together. We airmen had a meager showing, but I recognized some of the serious runners from the hospital. In fact, Air Force women took four of the top five times. I always wondered who the freaks were who wore costumes to the road races. Well, I suppose I must have passed some mental threshold of normal behavior, because I thought it would be a great idea to run the race in the leprechaun costume that arrived in a sweet care package. Of course I ran in armor, plates, and helmet; there is no reason to stop now! I ran with a fellow airman from the hospital, and I was impressed to learn the person I worked shoulder to shoulder with in the ER every day was a Viet Nam vet with a Purple Heart. I was very impressed and honored to be serving with him. The Army base commander attended the race, so I was able to represent and give him a view of Air Force style. I think I fit right in with the guy dressed as a Viking and the guy playing bagpipes. I finished the race in 69 minutes which seemed slow for only 6 miles. So many runners were surprised at their long times that the organizers rechecked the mileage and realized they had actually mapped out a seven-mile course, proving once again that "Army intelligence" is an oxymoron. It didn't matter. The Valentine's Day ten-kilometer race was only five-miles long, so it all evened out over the two races.

I'm sure I've mentioned how hard it is to have time alone here. Every work area is constantly occupied and in use. Last Tuesday when I was post-call, I took a long walk before dinner just to have some time to myself and think. I found a former Iraqi building with a tall chimney, and I climbed up the ladder to look around. From that perch, with a cool breeze blowing from the West over the Euphrates River in the distance, the base seemed so much more manageable and peaceful. I took some photos to make a panorama of the base. With all the drab industrial equipment it resembled a miniature Elizabeth, New Jersey. It's mostly the stacks of shipping containers that give that effect, but the smell of burning plastic and medical waste adds to the similarity.

On St. Patrick's Day, I made a surprise journey, and I will tell you 'twas my misfortune the trip wasn't to my local for a pint! I visited the gym to record my miles on my "Run to Baghdad" log. If you can run over 100 miles while you are stationed at Balad AB, you earn bragging rights and a free T-shirt stating "I ran to Baghdad". Some have gotten their shirt already, but I'm only halfway there. Of course, not everyone is running to Baghdad in armor. In the gym, I ran into intensivist Kevin, one of the critical care doctors. Did I know there was a sick three-year-old in the hospital who needed a medical attendant to get him out of the country? No, I did not. Need the info, people. This little guy had an infection called leishmaniasis. It is quite common in Iraq, and the following day when we described his symptoms to Dr. O. from the Balad Hospital, he said, "Hmm, that sounds like leishmaniasis." But for doctors from the United States, it is quite rare, and tougher to recognize. The eye cannot see what the mind does not know. Some of the soldiers get a milder form of the infection in the skin called the "Baghdad Boil" when they are bitten by sand flies. So, I visited the child. He had a bloated belly from the effects of the infection on his internal organs. He was hooked up to a breathing machine and had intravenous tubes going into him. His grandfather, a sheik, stood nearby and was ready to accompany him wherever he went.

After numerous phone calls and adjustments in plan, we came to the decision that he would travel to another facility in Iraq staffed by American military doctors, from which he had just come. I had the wonderful discovery that there were two Army pediatric surgeons in Iraq, and we discussed plans for this child. With the recommendations from chief of staff George, who is also an infectious diseases specialist, our two hospitals together determined a plan of treatment. The helicopter to transport the child was rapidly approaching, so I ran home to put on a desert camouflage uniform and get some gear. I checked out a weapon from our facility and, with the transport team, gathered up medical equipment, oxygen tanks, and medications to make the trip.

On the helipad, the prop wash swept waves of dust over us. The sound of the rotors and the earplugs we were wearing for hearing protection made communication by hand signals necessary. Under the direction of the pilot and helicopter medic, we approached the aircraft safely from the side and loaded little A., our crew, and A.'s grandfather into the helicopter. The sun had just set, and a pale yellow glow traced the outline of the horizon. The pilot gently lifted the Black Hawk off the helipad and quickly rose to altitude. The nose of the helicopter tipped down, we accelerated and banked a graceful arc to the right, and effortlessly left Balad Air Base behind. It was my first time outside of her walls in nearly two months. Our transportable ventilators could not be calibrated to the small breaths A. required, so for the entire half-hour flight I breathed for him by squeezing and relaxing a rubber bellows bag that drove oxygen into the tube down his throat. Even though he was small, he required such a high concentration of oxygen that I needed to turn the tanks to full blast to keep from mixing in ambient air. Intensivist Jon from the ICU gave him the medications necessary to keep him sedated. The pilot flew in complete darkness, using specialized goggles to see his instruments and the terrain below us. We kept the cabin dark to reduce our visibility from below and avoid disturbing the pilot's hypersensitive goggles. The only light was the orange screen of the monitor tracing out the child's heart rhythm and vital signs. I kept one hand on the ventilation bag and the other on the boy's chest to feel its rise and fall with each breath. Whenever we had to give medications, we used a dim blue light the pilot had given us that didn't interfere with his vision.

Underneath us, the glow of lights from small mud huts in fields splashed out onto dirt clearings. The dark, still surface of the Tigris River wound its way beneath us. Soon the fields gave way to streets and widely spaced homes. As we crossed over the city limits, we saw row after row of apartment housing beneath us and the unexpected sight of files of cars moving sluggishly in traffic. Our pilot turned and maneuvered over the hospital's landing zone and softly sank through the air to touch down. We had already nearly depleted our oxygen sypply, so I was relieved to see we had made it to our destination.

Things had gone so well up to this point for our delicate patient. As we exited the Black Hawk and loaded the stretcher on a four-wheeler for the short trip to the entrance of the hospital, my efforts to give baby A. his breaths became ineffective. His vital signs flagged and then failed. We rushed through the lobby, rode the elevator up to the intensive care unit, and rolled in. The nurses and technicians sprang into action. Army pediatric surgeon Eric was paged and joined our efforts. It was only through the quick action and skillful care of the fine members of the ICU team that we were able to stabilize the child, restore his vital signs to their normal values, and connect him to the life-support equipment. As A.'s circulation strengthened and his little feet became pink, expressions of relief and smiles spread across the faces of the team members.

It felt strange to walk through marbled halls and under high ceilings after having operated in a tent for two months. Pediatric surgeon Eric was nice enough to show us around a little, and took us to see two young girls he was treating for significant burns to their faces and upper bodies. It was a sight all too similar to my little burn ward at Balad. Their parents shook our hands and were so expressive of their gratitude, even to us as visiting doctors. The girls eyed us quietly and it was immediately obvious they were being kept comfortable and well cared for by the nursing staff. In the flurry of activity after our arrival, intensivist Jon and I missed our chance to ride back to Balad on the horse we came in on, as that Black Hawk had left while we were resuscitating A.. The sergeant on duty for medevac transportation was so helpful in getting the message out that two doctors needed a ride. We visited the temporary sleeping quarters, a tent ringed by tall date palms on a square of grass next to the hospital. We wandered over to the Morale, Welfare, and Recreation building to snack on some cashews and Pringles while talking with some other troops who were up late. They were trying to secure plastic over a hole in the wall to keep the neighborhood stray cats out of the building. As I was holding the chair a soldier was standing on to reach the hole, the transportation sergeant entered with the news she had found us a helicopter pilot willing to bring medical equipment back to Balad, the equipment being two wayward doctors!

As I flew back to my temporary home at Balad in the darkness and isolating noise of the helicopter, I stared out at the lights on the ground, each marking a home here, a family there. I prayed for peace and safety to come to both our countries. The reflection of a crescent moon shimmered as it danced on the surface of the river we were following home. Our pilot expertly touched down onto the helipad of our familiar little tent hospital and delivered us safely back to our station.

I have received more and more requests for medical care for Iraqi children. This week, a man brought his 18-month-old daughter to the gate. The guards keeping us safe then called to the hospital to ask if we would see her, and with her father, she came in. The girl was the size of a baby half her age and couldn't walk or crawl. But what I noticed first about her was the deep yellow jaundice coloring her eyes and skin. Some further testing confirmed she has a liver disease which I have treated in the United States, but usually before a baby is two-months-old. Left unchecked, it causes permanent liver damage and death within a few years. I had never seen a patient with this disease that old. She eyed me with fear, and cried when I examined her. But in her mother's arms, she looked around the room curiously, feeding herself a bottle. This family had been searching for help at the Iraqi hospitals, but they were sent to see the Americans. A patrol of soldiers met her parents at a town meeting and helped them get to our base. I know if I do nothing she will die, but the surgery itself is a risk of death. At her age, the damage to her liver might be permanent. I expressed this to the family and they are eager for any chance at survival. I will try my best to get her through it safely.

One boy visited for me to examine him after previous heart surgery. Last summer, patrolling soldiers sweeping through an Iraqi city discovered him. He had been burned with boiling water. When the previous doctors at our hospital took care of him, they realized he had a heart defect that had never been fixed. Through the donations of American citizens, he was flown to Tampa, FL and had successful heart surgery. When I met him, I found him to have an excellent heart, but upon examining him further I discovered he needed surgery for his gonads. It is just our good fortune to be deployed here with urologist Eddie, and we will be operating together on the boy this week.

Today another boy, a 15-year-old with a chronic lung disease, showed up at the gate. His father had a scrap of paper with my name scrawled on it. I spent the afternoon with him, doing tests not available elsewhere in the country. With the help of my fine colleagues in the lab, we were able improvise a sweat test for cystic fibrosis. I placed a plastic bag on this young man's hand to collect enough sweat to do the test. Our respiratory therapists educated the boy's father in ways to perform therapy to prolong the function of his damaged lungs and prevent episodes of pneumonia. We were also able to give him medications. As this deployment progresses, I find my mission is expanding to include some duties I never expected. I just hope we can help a few people out and leave knowing we did some good. Once I have walked by these children, I feel like I own a share in their fate.

I have been able to send S., the two-month-old baby with burns, home because she has done so well. Her sister, M., had been doing well and was healing her burns, but had a bad day today. She developed difficulty breathing and needed to be reconnected to the mechanical ventilator. I haven't figured out what caused this complication for her. It may be an infection, but I am frustrated I don't know why she has gotten worse.

I do also take care of adults! One gentleman was injured back in November. He lost part of his colon and part of his right hand. We are taking care of him now to help heal a bedsore on his back. When he went to surgery last week, he insisted I take his picture with the OR team so I would remember him. We told him not to worry. Since he has been cared for by two groups of American surgeons, he now has a famous backside we will not soon forget. His surgery went well, and he is up and walking around the hospital with strong strides. I got to meet his father and brother when they visited. Another of our former patients visited, and it was good to see him in better health. In spite of his three surgeries, he is back to full duties in his job as a soldier who is commanding troops in this area to keep it safe for us and the Iraqis living in Balad.

Thank you for all the goodies you have sent! We always have candy and snacks to nosh on. One fun present from surgeon Deb back home was temporary tattoos. She is commanding the surgeons back at my home station, and has always made sure the deployed surgeons know they are remembered and their families are fine. She probably intended them to be for the children, but anesthetist Annie and I couldn't resist the urge to get tattys. She looks tough with hers, but I just look like Bowser on Sha Na Na!

Anything that helps make the days pass by faster around here is welcome! We have buds on the rose bush behind The Swamp. Hopefully, I will have a blossoming flower in the desert soon. My cilantro is growing in the sandbags around my hooch, and soon I will have a few sprigs to bring to the chow hall. I'm doing my best to keep my haircut squared away myself with the clippers I brought. It's not that I'm too busy or too cheap to go to the barber, I'm just too lazy! After all, with the cut I've chosen, there aren't too many skill points needed.

Around base, I try not to walk by any dangerous or precarious situation without either fixing it or letting someone know. I walked by the oxygen tanks, and somehow, an aluminum tent brace had fallen on the tubing. That was an easy fix. In the makeshift scramble to make this busy base work, however, I see many examples of things that just don't look right. The most interesting is the line of sandbags covering an electrical wire that crosses the sidewalk, enters the sewer on one side of the road, and emerges from the sewer grate on the other side of the road. All it takes is a phone call to get most of this stuff taken care of. There is just so much activity on base. We can't expect it to always be in perfect condition, but for everyone's safety, we have to keep our eyes open so we don't walk by an accident that could have been prevented.

Well, my eyes grow dim. Thank you for remembering us and sending us your good thoughts and prayers. We are doing our best to look out for each other so everyone gets home safe. This busy little city of a base has more than enough to keep us occupied until we catch that ride home. Be well, and be gentle with one another.

Peace,

Chris

14

"Sad News"

Just below the surface
Thursday 24 MAR 2005

Dear Friends,

I have been caring for a two-year-old girl with burns named M. for the past month. In spite of heroic efforts from the team of doctors, nurses, and techs taking care of her, she passed away tonight at 18:50. I knew her long enough to learn that her favorite stuffed animal was a pink bear, she loved chips and snacks, and her giggles brought joy to her mother and father. Nearly everyone in our hospital from the ER, OR, ICU, wards, respiratory, pharmacy, nutrition, laboratory, chaplain, and others has had a hand in this sweet girl's treatment. It is only through the hard work of those caring people that she was able to survive as long as she did. For the past four days, she has been critically ill on life support. Her young heart gave out after enduring much more than one with less will to live could. We cleaned her and wrapped her in pads and a blanket. Her parents were

71

unable to visit today due to heightened security on the base. We contacted her father's military unit, and our guards arranged for him to pass through security this evening. One of our ambulance medics picked him up at the gate along with M.'s older brother and her uncle. Our translator helped me speak to them, but there was little to say. I carried M. out to the ambulance. After the men in her family climbed in, I placed her in her uncle's arms. I lost sight of them as the Humvee ambulance doors swung shut.

If you pray, please remember M.'s family in your prayers. Thank you for all your prayers for M. and the toys and treats you sent. She is not the first child I have seen die, and I know I am not so fortunate that she will be the last. Tomorrow, I will go back to work and try to help the others who come my way. But tonight I am broken.

I will write again soon.

Chris

15

"Dustoff, Again"

The helipad that never closes
Friday 25 MAR 2005

Hello again, my friends,

Thank you so much for your emails, support, and prayers for M.'s family. I hope they can find solace after this tragedy. It comforted me greatly to receive your good wishes. The compassion of my friends here, especially surgeon Brett and neurosurgeon Lee, helped me prop myself up again. However, we didn't have much time to reflect on M.

I had been in my hooch for an hour and hadn't even undressed when I heard the approach of a helicopter. After it took off, two more landed in quick succession. My pager went off, I pulled on my gear, and jumped on my bike to pedal the short distance to the hospital. The emergency room was abuzz with four injured Iraqi policemen surrounded by team members methodically checking vital signs, starting intravenous lines, taking x-rays, and dressing wounds. They had been injured in an attack by a vehicle-borne IED and there were more to come. Our hospital had activated the mass casualty recall.

The page went out for all personnel to return to the hospital to assist. This happens when the wounded are expected to overwhelm the capabilities of the hospital. There is always a surgeon and anesthetist or anesthesiologist in the hospital prepared to immediately start an operation on a severely injured patient. When the full team is called back, we can simultaneously perform six operations. The whole show is orchestrated by surgeon Dave, who takes the role of trauma czar. He directs the flow of patients and assigns personnel to tasks. All information flows to him so he knows our status and capabilities at all times. He has to make split second decisions and sometimes has to weigh the risks to one patient against the risks to another.

Over the next eight hours we received 19 patients, 10 of whom proceeded to the operating room. The military hospital in Baghdad became overwhelmed to the point that they diverted their incoming traffic to us. The rhythmic stutter of the arriving, waiting, and departing Black Hawks and Chinooks continuously filled the tents with noise. We would no sooner finish one case than it was time to start another. I washed out wounds and removed jagged fragments of shrapnel. I worked with surgeon Todd to repair a severed artery to a policeman's hand. I explored necks for injuries to the blood supply to the brain, and I sewed the ragged shreds of an ear back together. I splinted broken bones with orthopedic Brian. In the other two operating rooms it was the same scene, as our team of highly skilled and practiced airmen patched up the handiwork of a suicide bomber.

After staying late with M. yesterday and then operating late tonight, I fell asleep on the couch in the middle of the hallway. I awakened as shafts of morning sunlight slipped through the gaps in the tent and brightened my vision. I had slept through half of morning rounds. Our team walked from ward to ward as a group to visit each patient and ensure they were safe and responding to the therapy we had chosen. Then it was back to work—changing dressings, removing tubes, arranging airevac flights for injured Americans, and on to the OR for the scheduled cases of the day. I've escaped the hospital to take a breather tonight, but Brian the general surgeon is still holding down the fort and cleaning up the last few injuries we detected on morning rounds.

There is no way we could handle this onslaught of critically injured soldiers without working as a seamlessly integrated team. Under the stress of working hard, sometimes we need to vent the pressure. Last week we celebrated the halfway point of our deployment with the classic ritual of American leisure, a barbecue! We passed the kitty and anesthesiologist Bob on the CCAT (Critical Care Air Transport) team, who flies critically ill patients to the military hospital in Germany, picked up a couple of coolers of meat and flew them back to us. The OR crew did an impressive job arranging packing and instrument containers into a picnic area in the gravel lot behind the hospital. The smell of roasting pork from the grill next to the Cadillacs, likely a rare smell in the land of Mohammed, was a welcome change from the usual smells of LSA Anaconda. We drank near-beer and grinned at each other with mouths full. Here we were in a war zone, 100 yards away from a guarded perimeter meant to keep out those with a will to kill us, and we were cooking out! For just a short while, we felt like kings and queens of our domain, as if we might have even chosen to come here and have such a good time. The suffering and critical demands of the ill paused briefly while we recharged. Shortly after the sun turned the sky orange and rosy hues, the party dissipated as helicopters brought more wounded men to our door. By the way, Gloria's Jalapeno Mustard and Foo's Fire were liberally applied to the tasty German bratwurst.

One treasured component of our cadre has been the highly capable doctors and nurses of the Australian Defense Forces. Counting among them an orthopedic surgeon, anesthesia tech, intensive care unit doctors and nurses, and ER staff, they have provided an essential part of our ability to care for sick patients. Today we bid farewell to their group as they completed their tour and departed Balad. As they shouldered weapons and donned armor to head out to the airstrip, I freely admit I was jealous! I will just have to hang in there a couple more months before I take my flight home. The Australians arrived before our contingent, and worked side by side with the Air Force group before us. They were seasoned and confident by the time we arrived, and did a lot to allay our fears and get us up to speed on the particulars of performing surgery in a tent. We exchanged addresses and embraces as we smiled at the memories of facing down challenges together, as well as the possibilities of reunion on either of two continents far away from Mortaritaville.

However, we are not to be completely bereft of the favorable influences of the countrymen from down under; their replacements arrived a week ago! And if initial impressions hold true, this group will be just as energetic, entertaining, and capable as the last. With the arrival of the new Australians last week, they invited the Americans to participate in the rededication of their recreational lounge, "The Camel Club". It lies in an extreme corner of the hospital compound, which in turn occupies an edge of the base so it is practically outside the gate. I suppose that is what can be expected from frontiersmen of the Outback. We had a wonderful time welcoming the new arrivals under the cascading leaves of a tall eucalyptus tree behind the Camel Club. Our own commander surgeon Chuck presided over a ribbon cutting, and inside, the Australian chaplain performed a blessing as he scattered water from Australia with a sprig of willow leaves. The addition of a touristy carved wooden camel from the local bazaar behind the PX made the scene complete.

Before things got so crazy today, we were able to perform some humanitarian work. I previously mentioned a boy who visited to have me check out his healing from a heart operation performed last year in Tampa, FL. Last week, urologist Eddie and I were able to correct a congenital problem with his gonads. The day after surgery, he mirrored his father's broad smile and played with the toy car kindly donated by one of you back home. He looked better after surgery than I'm sure I will if I ever need an operation. The operation will reduce the chance of a dangerous cancer growing unchecked, and will give him a better chance that one day he may have a boy or girl of his own. Eddie doesn't usually work with children, but I was very impressed as I watched his delicate work, and certainly picked up a few tricks from him. Eddie has a great photo album with recorded audio messages from his beautiful kids to go with each picture. I know his family misses him and will be so happy to have him back.

Our team has a player on the injured list! Orthopedic PA Tim was conducting a mission-essential maneuver on his mountain bike when the ground approached him at excessive speed and he suffered a separated shoulder. Our wounded eagle has his wing in a sling, but it doesn't slow him down. He is splinting and casting one-handed in the clinic and performing repetitions of physical therapy exercises between patients. I think our

patients are feeling a new solidarity with him. Our Australian orthopedic surgeon, Gregor, responded with the ballad *Mulga Bill's Bicycle*, in which Mulga Bill suffered a similar fate when he abandoned his trusty horse for a bicycle. I'll admit the event has given me pause over the bike jumps and Yugos. Maybe I'll try something safer, like airborne training.

Holy week is upon us. As I celebrate Christ's death and rebirth, I am closer than I have ever been to the Holy Land where the events actually happened. I am heartened to know I am loved and guided through the good times and the bad. Though I am far from my family whom I love so much, and I simply ache for missing them, I am so thankful and blessed to have them and to know each night they go to bed in a safer land far away from this mess. I pray for the rebirth of peace in this troubled country, and an end to the tide of broken bodies coming through our doors. I look forward to the day our presence here becomes obsolete.

Peace may seem unexpected or even ludicrous here, but I have faith in my heart it is possible in spite of our stumbling path. And on a more secular note, thank you for the generous gift of your decorations; I hope the Easter Bunny visits all of your houses! Have a joyful and peaceful Easter, warm in the embrace of your loved ones.

Peace, over and out.

Chris.

16

"Holidays in the Sun"

Moustache Junction, Iraq
Wednesday, 30 MAR 2005

Hello again, friends,

I have so much to say, but I really cannot put it into words. It is quite simple, but perhaps the intensity with which I feel it makes it seem like it couldn't come out clearly. The closest I can come is, "No matter how fascinating the events of my life over here are, and how staggeringly humbled and fortunate I feel to have the honor of caring for our nation's heroes, I still can't stand this patch of dirt and want to get home to the people who love me best and I love best, but fast!" That does not sound quite right, but it will have to do.

Easter was quite eventful, but first let me tell you about today. Now it is 01:00, I'm in my hooch, and I'm listening to Bob Marley sing *Satisfy My Soul*. "When you hold me tight, you make me feel all right." Hmm, guess of whom that makes me think? Meredith, ti amo. I might get to talk to my twin brother

Vinny tonight, and that is one good reason to stay up. He's not really my twin, he's more my bluesman and lawyer, but since we were born about eight hours apart, we've felt like we might as well be twins.

Since it is after midnight, I actually will be talking about yesterday, the 29th. I nearly overslept, which is nothing new, but scrambled to work on the trusty Mega Flex mountain bike generously loaned to me by dietician Heidi. Rounds were rounds. We visit all of the patients every morning to make sure things are going well. When we have all the medical team collected we number near 30, so it is quite an entourage. I performed a brief operation to clean the wounds of a severely injured American so he could be prepared for his flight to Germany. (I'll tell you more about him later, too.) Then I settled in to the important but unpleasant task of preparing M&M.

I know some of you might not know M&M as more than the tasty chocolate in the candy shell, but in my world it stands for "morbidity and mortality", and it is a conference in which doctors present their mistakes and failures to their peers. Some failures are not failures, because we all are born to die, and sometimes not even the most skilled doctor can stop that train. In this vein, some failures of medicine are actually a merciful turn for the better of the patient. Still, to learn from our mistakes and to allow others to learn the lesson the easy way, and try to create a collective experience and wisdom, we gather to discuss our errors and bad outcomes. A sociologist, Shapira, described M&M conference as a chance to "forgive and remember" in his book of the same title. He wrote it after following a group of surgeons around a hospital for a few months. The book is a fascinating view of my world, and he also described perfectly the paradox that a physician must actually make mistakes in order to learn enough to become a good doctor.

You can imagine I had stimulus enough to grow grumpy (and even grumplicious) as I sat there trying to recreate the sequence of events leading to our group's errors, and even the deaths of our patients. Half the battle is chasing down the details of each case from the other surgeons, as well as finding lost x-rays and pictures from surgery. Included among these was the story of my patient M., who, as many of you know, is a child who recently died in my care after suffering severe burns. On top of all this, I was convinced the air handling system was somehow set wrong and was pumping superheated air onto the back of my neck. I was feeling far too sweaty as I labored away at the computer for hours. Finally, with the help of some of my partners, I had the data rounded up, and headed out in armor to the surprise that the temperature had risen to 85 degrees and it wasn't the heating system that was torturing me. This was different! Anything different is good! I was very happy to have some sign of hot weather coming. It is one thing to grind away indoors in the heat, but when I'm outdoors I would prefer to bathe in the climate of Texas. Call it just another nugget of homesickness. Truth be told, we are expecting the temperature to surpass 110 degrees before we leave, hot even by San Antonio standards. I'm sure I'll take back my words then. I came home (that's my temporary home, the hooch) to a new and exciting sound; a front-end loader was pushing gravel around my "front yard". Since it seems the rainy season may just have ended, they have delivered better drainage precisely when we don't need it anymore. It was thought provoking, but quite consistent with the systematic program of FUBAR, which for you non-military types stands for "Fouled-up beyond all recognition". (See, it wasn't as bad as you thought!)

After dropping off my uniform in the hooch, I suited up in PT gear and armor, strapped on a liter of water in my Camelbak, and headed out for an eight-mile run. It was perfect timing. As I ran back from one of the gates, the sun set, and I got to run the last four miles under a dusky sky lit with streaks of yellow, orange, and pink, miraculously visible through the dust and chemical gas being emitted from burning garbage. I hooked up with orthopedic surgeon Rick and orthopedic PA Bill for a mile in the middle, but Bill was leading us on a much more tactical pace than I was used to. I dropped back to finish an easy final three. I'm very used to running in helmet, Kevlar, and plates, but I wonder if it will be too much to swim in when the pool opens. At least it will give me a nasty advantage in the upcoming biggest splash contest.

Well, I've still got a lot to get you through in this letter, so I'll get back where I should be. Sometimes you just can't get to the stock until you skim off the schmaltz.

Easter started well. I was grumpy (big surprise, usual reason). I hadn't slept the night before. My insomnia has not disappeared even after two months. I went to the hospital early and decided to start the day the way every teacher I have ever had said was the right way, with a big breakfast. I was delighted to find in the usual chafing dish reserved for dingy, cracked, smallish hard-boiled eggs an eye-popping surprise of dyed Easter eggs! (Remember? Anything different is good!).

So I was grumpy because I was away from family. (Stay with me, this isn't more complaining, like it seems to be.) But Easter Sunday I started out grumpy because I knew I would be missing home more than usual without the special ceremonies and celebrations of a happy holiday with loved ones. As the day flowed, I found that Easter in Iraq was different, but not wholly bad. To explain why, because it wasn't as obvious to me as it should have been, it was saved by the fact that I was with my special, close, powerful deployed family. We are in this together. We have seen fire and we have seen rain. I know everyone has seen fire and rain, but we saw it together and we saw it over here. I trust these people. I know they can turn in the goods; I have seen them do it day after day. They have worked miracles with duct tape and 550 cord, and they have gently held the hands of dying men and gone on to snatch them back from the brink. When I have stumbled, they have caught my elbow. When I have sunk into a funk they have teased me back into a good mood. They have given me chocolate to keep the Dementors away. So my Easter would be different, but it still would be celebration of the risen Lord who made this life so precious, with people I have come to care about very much in the past two months.

I operated in the morning. Surgery took me past the time for Mass, but that was nothing new because duties at the hospital had gotten in the way of attending any of the holy week ceremonies. It wasn't the first time since entering training for surgery that I worshiped in my own way, at a slightly more intimate altar in the OR. I'm thankful both Mom and Teddy sent me passages to read each day so I had a chance for brief spiritual reflection. After helping out at the hospital until the afternoon, I went home for a nap.

I got up after three hours of sleep, and in spite of my body's arguments to the contrary, I dragged myself into armor and out of the hooch. That night at 19:30 was the spectacular Easter Party and March Moustache Madness judging. This event would restore my faith. The hospital DFAC (dining facility) was gaily decorated in pastels, eggs, and bunnies, along with mountains of candy and cake on the table. The room was packed with my happy comrades. I was a bit nervous about the competition, so I sipped a coffee to steel my resolve. I snuck off to put on my bunny ears and tail, as I thought a few props might give me the edge I needed to nose out in front of the competition. I had considered wearing only my costume and a Speedo, but fortunately better judgment prevailed, even without Meredith around to keep me from walking off the cliff.

The competition was serious. We were each given numbers and called up in pairs, which was an ingenious way to pit us against each other. I had seen this technique used in interviews for the pediatric surgery fellowship at Chicago Memorial Hospital, and it was cutthroat! Early on, surgeon Todd set the bar quite high with a winning performance. Contestants who were absent, because there was an operation going on at the same time, were displayed to the audience and the judges via digital images on a laptop. We even got one of the Iraqi translators to join the fray, and he looked like he got a kick out of parading his moustache for the ladies at the judges' table.

Finally it was my turn. I was called up with orthopedic Rick, a formidable opponent with his bushy red and brown specimen. I felt like I was in front of Randy, Paula, and Simon. I knew I had to pull out all the stops. I reached back, channeled the Purrfect Angelz dance show, and showed off my best disco moves. I even gave my tail (bunny tail, that is!) to nurse Barbara from the OR! And then my turn was over. It was up to the judges, and orthopedic Brian looked like he was Price Waterhouse at the Academy Awards as he tabulated the results. Even if I didn't win, at least I made five dollars for my dancing. If this surgery thing ever doesn't work out, I might have a backup.

A group of us slipped out for some night air to escape the pressure. We climbed to the roof of The Swamp and talked under the light of a waning moon. The stars twinkled over the fields along the Tigris. The lights of Balad city smudged a shallow glow on the horizon. From the runway, we heard the roar of an F-16 thrusting skyward, followed quickly by the takeoff of her wingman. I realized that I might not be home, but I was among friends. One of the techs asked me advice on how to get into medical school. I felt complimented to be asked and I gave him some tips, as well as my number back home with an offer to help further back in San Antonio. I looked at the silvery moon, and I was jealous she got to travel over my home night after night while I was stuck here. It was approaching noon in Texas, and I sent out my wishes and prayers that Meredith and the boys were happy, and also my promises that I would hurry home soon. The call rang out from the hospital in the night air—the results were ready.

Could it be true? Could there be an award for me? My answer was the certificate attesting I had won the Ron Jeremy Look-Alike category. Oh, happy day! I celebrated by taking a much needed shower and shaving my little friend off my lip!

I called home and was so happy to hear Meredith's voice. It is like a drug, and I go into withdrawal if I go too long without hearing her. She and the boys were having a peaceful Easter at home, and hearing each of them on the phone just made me smile wider and wider. I added Easter to the list of things we would celebrate when were together again. I also called Mom and Dad in Connecticut, and my brothers had me laughing as usual. The only one I couldn't reach was Amanda, but I sent out my good wishes, thoughts, prayers, and love to her from Iraq.

By this time, Midnight Chow was up so I hoofed it the quarter mile to DFAC 2. The place was brimming with diners and decorated to the hilt. Some of you have seen these bizarre decorations already in my friend Lee's letter, but I think they are extraordinary enough to deserve a second mention. The tables were lined up tavern-style with pastel purple paper and Easter centerpieces. Eggs and streamers hung from the low ceiling. The cafeteria line was a carnival of decorations, the most remarkable ones carved from colored fruits. There were strange beasts and festive colors. There was a custard Golgotha, complete with three lime crosses nestled behind scraggly-armed baked bread trees. And the *piece de resistance*, a tiny watermelon rind Jesus crucified with toothpicks onto a bas-relief cross. Although it might seem inappropriate at first, and probably was, on further thought I considered that the rind of a sweet fruit was a fitting symbol of the fragile human shell that Christ took on to save us. I don't know if the extravagant display was simply the best approximation the local Muslim workers could deduce for how Easter should be celebrated. Alternatively, it may represent how another Christian culture marks the holiday, perhaps in the Philippines. Whatever the explanation, it was great!

I tucked in to a dinner of Chicken Cordon Bleu, Swiss steak, mashed potatoes, and a favorite dessert for a guy who doesn't like dessert, blueberry cobbler. And if that wasn't enough to be thankful for on Easter, I reached into the ammo pouch on my vest and pulled out a treasure: a bottle of Marie Sharp's Habanero Pepper Sauce (Proud Product of Belize). You might have thought I had abandoned my pursuit of the perfect military meal and hot sauce pairing, but the quest goes on! The Chicken Cordon Bleu is actually one of the DFAC's more palatable creations, probably because it is assembled far from Iraq, deep frozen, and then reheated for use after arrival on our dear LSA Anaconda. The usual pairing for the Sunday night steak dinner is lobster tail or snow crab legs, for which I had packed the Marie Sharp's, but the chicken would do well. The steak was quickly dispatched with some A-1, a straightforward and reliable choice, as long as the cut didn't have too much gristle. Some nights, you can still see where the jockey was hitting it, but for Easter I was blessed with a tender cut. Marie Sharp's bright personality shone through the bottle in its cheery orange hue (carrots), and the gold foil-adorned label promised "Fiery Hot". Opening the lid, the bouquet of lime and garlic leaped out, and the sauce poured fast and smooth. The taste was a celebration of lime and onion, with well-blended themes of garlic and pleasant warmth from the habaneras. It went well with the butter and cheese of the chicken dish and made for a memorable meal.

But back to a less pleasant topic, my poor sleep hygiene. My problem is I am still retaining the rhythms of home. It is probably because that is where my heart is. So many moments in the day, I glance at the time on my pager (yes, we have those over here!) and I imagine what my sweetie and the boys are doing. I tried getting up early to force an early bedtime. I considered Da Vinci sleep. (My concept of what that is comes from *Seinfeld*'s Kramer, who tried to stay on a cycle of one hour of sleep followed by three hours of work.) Even I could see that was ridiculous. From the outside, my next direction might seem strange, but I was desperate. I decided to try and reverse my sleep/wake cycle, since I was staying up every night anyway. I stayed up the few hours after Midnight Chow until it was time to go to work. I went to the hospital, rounded, and did a few small operations, including a short but challenging re-operation for a recurrence of a groin hernia in a young soldier surgeon Mike found in clinic. I used a technique called a "plug and patch", in which the weak area in the muscle is strengthened by placing mesh in the body; it looks a lot like the material in a window screen. We have no plugs over here, so I had to build one out of a flat piece of mesh. The final product looked a lot like a badminton shuttlecock (or birdie, for those who use that term, but I just like writing "shuttlecock"). As he woke up, disoriented, the patient reached out for a hug and got a warm embrace from my dear friend anesthetist Annie. I went to my temporary home and climbed into bed at 11:00, planning to sleep eight hours and wake in the evening to stay awake all night as usual, but this time after a decent chunk of sleep.

Of course, we all know what happens to the best laid plans of mice and men. Two hours later, I awoke bleary eyed to the repeated beeping of my pager. The clock indicated it had been going off for half an hour. I assembled a version of the uniform and shambled over to the outdoor phone mounted on the concrete barriers protecting our hooches. Could I come in please, there was a child in the clinic whose parents wanted me to see him. This was the first day he could come in, because the base gates had been locked down since Thursday before Easter. The doctors and doctor's spouses among you all know the answer, so I picked up my armor and rode my loaner Mega Flex mountain bike to the hospital to meet A. He is a nine-year-old boy, and his family came to know of me because his uncle is one of our translators. I sat down with the translator, the boy, and his father. From the time he was a toddler, he has had a problem with his bottom, in which every time he has a bowel movement, part of his intestine comes out and has to be tucked back in by hand. At first his parents did it, but he has since learned to do it on his own. He is a beautiful healthy boy the same age as my oldest son, and throughout the interview he smiled at me broadly. His mood is happy and open; that will change when he needs an intravenous catheter placed, but we are not there yet. I know this problem he has; I can help. I ask my questions, "Does his waste float on water in the toilet?" Hesitation. The men discuss the topic in Arabic without giving me an answer through several exchanges. The translator turns to me and says, "Umm, they do not have that type of a toilet with water, so they do not know." After further questions and a physical exam, it seems reasonably clear he has a condition called prolapse of the rectum, probably because he has trouble absorbing the wheat protein in bread. I explain a minor procedure I can do that day under a light anesthetic, and after going over the risks, we are in agreement. I take A. over to the ER for his lab tests and the aforementioned IV.

I am 7000 miles from home, I have had five hours sleep in two days, but I am happy. I am doing what I was trained to do, and I have found a condition I can fix. I am going about the arrangements for the procedure in the OR when the sound of helicopter rotors fills the air overhead, and I can feel my heart drop as I am forcibly reminded of where I am and the real reason I was sent here. Now, I have strayed a bit from the formula of the "happy, sad, happy" sandwich of events in my updates, but honestly I don't feel like I can control how it comes out. I like to think that no matter how horrible the events I see here, I can find in them some grace of compassion, bravery, or even just the familiarity of humanity. So bear with me through this and I will try. And don't worry about A., he does eventually make it to the OR.

My slim hope that I would be able to continue with A.'s procedure uninterrupted is quickly squashed as I see three young American soldiers wheeled in, the faces of the medics grim, and a trail of blood splashing on the floor as they traverse the ER. Surgeon Dave takes the first one. The patient's skin is an ashen grey, the color of the cement floor tinged with a faint purple. His eyes are sunken and stare out at nothing, and his mouth is open and dry as he moans and speaks softly. The blood is coming from his legs and seeps through the mesh fabric of the NATO stretcher. Dave and surgeon Todd quickly go to work, and he soon has large intravenous catheters and is receiving an emergency transfusion. With the team, they continue to remove the tatters of his clothing and examine him for wounds. One leg is severely damaged, with shards of shattered bone visible; the other has several wounds into the muscle.

I attend to the next man. He looks good, a little shaken up, but awake and strong with good color. What's his name? It begins with S., a common American name. He is only injured in his left leg. A fragment of metal has entered the thigh on one side and come so close to shooting out of the other side I can see it bulging under the skin. The metal was so heated from the explosion which wrecked their Humvee that it has singed the skin from the inside, and there is a patch of burned skin over the lump of metal. I lift his leg and he flinches and cries out. The bone seems broken. I splint it and move on to the third man.

The nurses and techs have already undressed him and started an intravenous catheter. He is hurting but still talking. "How are my men?" he asks. He and the other two look like they are barely out of their teens. This one is the Humvee commander who was in charge of the vehicle when it hit the IED. He used to be a tanker and wishes he still was. I'll bet! I tell him I've just come from S. and he is doing well. "They are both named S.," he replies. I lie and tell him they both are going to be fine. He is worried the first man is going to lose an eye; I'm concerned he is going to lose his life.

I look over his injuries. A fragment of Humvee the size and shape of a Swingline stapler has embedded in his right arm. The flesh is torn away, and I can see the shiny ends of the bones of his elbow where the joint has broken open. I will find out later that this man first applied a tourniquet to his own shoulder, and then crawled to where the first man lay bleeding to death. With his one good arm, he tightened tourniquets around his charge's thighs. He then talked to him while waiting for the choppers to arrive. I give him morphine while I put him through the painful task of removing the fabric of his uniform sleeve from around the embedded chunk of metal.

Surgeon Dave is in charge as the trauma czar. He directs me to take the first man to the OR. He needs an amputation of the left leg, and the wounds on the right leg cleaned. We hurry the first man into the OR, and I turn care of the Humvee commander over to Todd. We park the stretcher next to the OR table and get ready to move the soldier over. I have performed amputations since I was a surgical intern. Often, they were on aging veterans who suffered gangrene caused by clogged arteries. The operations were scheduled, and it was apparent to everyone, including the men, that the rotten leg was doing them no good. Amputation was a chance to get rid of a festering infection and get out of the hospital. I hadn't performed an amputation at Balad yet, because the orthopedic surgeons performed most of them. These patients had come in so fast and so sick, the orthopedic surgeons hadn't time to arrive at the hospital yet. I looked down at this young man's muscular legs and saw his left leg was blown apart above the knee, attached only by a strip of skin and gristle. I took out a pair of shears (exactly like the one I keep in my kitchen to quarter chickens), and cut his leg off with two snips through that isthmus of skin.

We moved him to the table, and after his skin was prepped with iodine, neurosurgeon Todd helped me find the stumps of severed arteries in his thigh to stop the bleeding. We cut away dead chunks of muscle and cracked off the sharp shards of his thighbone until the cut end was short and smooth. Anesthetist Jeff kept him alive by pumping blood and warmed fluids into the catheters surgeon

Dave and surgeon Todd had placed. We cleaned the wounds on his right leg, and when orthopedic Brian arrived, he taught me how to use pins and graphite bars to stabilize his broken right thigh bone. While we were working, surgeon Todd brought the man with the injured arm to the other table in the same OR. That strong brave soldier who saved the life of the man on the table in front of me needed to have his arm amputated. All three men survived. They were wheeled to the intensive care unit to await evacuation to Germany.

I went and found A., who was thirsty and impatient to eat, like any nine-year-old would be if he went without food and water all day. I brought him to the OR and performed the minor procedure on his bottom while anesthetist Bruce kept him unconscious with anesthetic gas. On the way to the OR, the child forgot his fears when he got to pick out a beanie baby and a John Deere tractor from our collection of donated toys. As I took care of the child, I tried not to think of the two young men down the hall who face a long climb to rebuild their lives missing a limb.

It was 19:00. I changed out of bloody scrubs and donned armor for the short walk home in the dark. The soldiers' blood had stained my tan boots red. I fell into bed and didn't rise for twelve hours.

I suppose I could state the obvious. I thank God those brave men survived what could have been lethal injuries. I am proud that the assembled expertise at our hospital made the difference between sending home corpses in flag-draped boxes and sending home three young heroes with their whole lives ahead of them, starting with rehabilitation in an all-too experienced military medical system. I see the Iraqis walking proudly in a country governed by a body they elected, as Iraqi and American soldiers work side by side to shake out the remains of a violent insurgency. Still, I want it over now. Why can't the last death really be the last one! Therein lies the rub. I wish they didn't have to keep getting injured, but as long as they do, we will be here to patch them up.

That brings us back to yesterday. It was much quieter by comparison. The eight-mile run did me much good. I had a nice dinner with surgeon Pete, who is running CCAT (Critical Care Air Transport) missions now like anesthetist Bob, who has a daughter in the same class as my son. It is now 05:50 and I am almost done. A. did wonderfully after his procedure and went home today. He and his father were very happy with the results. With this warm weather, my sandbag herb garden is flourishing, and I'm sure the sun will burn the leaves if I don't keep up with the watering. Even the tomatoes and peppers have sprouted. Lastly, the rose that neurosurgeon Todd and I have been tending behind The Swamp now has a beautiful, deep red blossom, so we have our desert rose. I send it home to you, Meredith, with a promise that I will follow soon. If you are still there, I thank you for listening. Every day, I am reminded how wonderful our country is and how precious is every life. I am thankful for yours. I hope I am doing well enough to be worthy of this uniform I wear, and your trust.

Love life and have fun!

Chris

17

"Hello Mudder, Hello Fadder"

Camp Balada
Wednesday, 6 APR 2005

Dear Friends,

Hello again, and I do hope this letter finds you well. The weather is clear and temperate, and we are going about our business in smooth routine. I must thank you for the many kind letters and generous care packages I have received. I try to send a letter or email to personally show my gratitude for remembering us. I have received so many snacks and useful items, much more than I could ever consume or use on my own. Luckily, there are always visitors to the hospital who could use a bite to eat, so there has been good opportunity to share this bounty. In fact, our commander had to remind us to police up our surgeons' area, because a broad display of Easter candy was threatening to interrupt the traffic of stretchers from the emergency room.

A number of poignant events have occurred since we last conversed, but first I wanted to share the overriding impression I have had recently that I am attending some bizarre variant of the activity camps I used to attend as a child. Receiving care packages and other details make this seem less like a war and more like slee-pover camp. Like any camp, life runs on a routine of scheduled rise and shine, and give God your glory, glory, and then on to an agenda of activities.

You've heard me tell of the different DFACs, which offer high cafeteria eating. We gather in small groups at our hooches and march over the DFACs. We wash our hands in turn with the Fairy brand soap and then queue up for brown stuff or tan stuff over rice. The beverage dispensers have iced tea, sweet tea, red bug juice, and green bug juice. Then we sit at long tables and plan out our activities for the day, or tell tales of victories over other groups of campers in competitions.

This feeling of attending a summer camp has grown stronger since the pools have opened. There is a majestic 50-meter outdoor pool with three diving plat-forms. The highest is 10-meters, a daunting height from which to stare down at the water and taunting friends. After completing duties at the hospital, I joined Team Huffy at the Army gymnasium and biked the short distance to the pool. Team Huffy is the orthopedic group taken to mountain bikes, and a few outside riders like myself. It's a rough gang, and we can count a few nasty scrapes and a separated shoulder among our battle wounds. We dropped our gear at the side of the pool and laid out on chaise lounges, slowly basting in the sun. Many tattoos were on display as we watched the young soldiers tumble off the 10-meter plat-form, making up for what they lacked in technique with fanfare and bravado. Orthopedic PA Tim performed an impressive back flip, made more so by the fact he was nursing a wounded arm. I managed a one and one quarter flip off the high dive, which felt as painful as it sounds. As we lay in the sun, with the water drying on our skin in the warm breeze wafting across the central plains of Iraq, I couldn't help but think that war is hell.

In summer camp style, the grand opening of the pools was marked by a luau and competitions. We were all proud that anesthetist Annie won a grass skirt in the limbo contest, proving herself to be one of the most flexible anesthetists you could ever work with, both in the operating room and when there is a limbo pole to dance under. Orthopedic Rick should have won the biggest splash contest, but he was robbed because the judging was by popular opinion, not any scientific measurement of the 30-foot plume of water his jackknife form sent into the air.

Chief Scott organized us into two squads for the 200-meter medley swim, and one of our groups took second place. I think we could have taken the leaders, but we took into account the winning Army foursome brought their M-16's to the pool. Intimidation may have been a factor. I displayed some promise for a future in private practice by winning the treasure dive, when I collected the high-scoring number of 42 coins from the bottom of the 12-foot deep indoor pool. Anyone who has completed a nine-year residency knows you learn to hold your breath and just get the job done.

What camp would be complete without bugs? We haven't seen the sand flies yet, but I still have gotten no end of consultations to biopsy soldiers' skin lesions to detect signs of the leishmaniasis infection they spread. Houseflies have started to present themselves in greater numbers, even in the operating rooms, in spite of our efforts to screen the entrances and provide positive air flow. Ophthalmologist Augie was working in the operating room when a fly landed right on the eye he was repairing. It must have been a peculiar sight under the high powered operating microscope he uses for his delicate work. The ants are in breeding season, and the winged kings and queens have been breezing about in clouds. I found a pair getting personal on the sandbags outside my window. I saw a sight reminiscent of home when I noticed a ladybug snacking on the cilantro I have been growing.

If we have anything akin to camp counselors, it would be the military police and guards patrolling the perimeter and keeping us safe. They enforce the rules, little things like, say, don't jog along the perimeter where snipers could take a pot shot at you. At the DFAC's, they ensure no one brings a backpack into the dining hall, as was used at Mosul in a suicide bombing. They stand guard over the detainees and enemy prisoners of war we treat in our hospital. When a detainee is well enough to be transferred to another facility in Iraq, they escort them and keep the medevac crew safe on the ride. As a recovering detainee left our hospital, he was flanked by one of the helicopter pilots and the transporting guard, slung shotgun and numerous shells adorning his armor.

As for arts and crafts at this summer camp, we unfortunately have no shortage of work in the OR. As usual, our activity comes and goes in swells of helicopters landing with injured patients. Recently, there was an attack on an American-controlled detention facility. The attackers, who used vehicle borne IED's and mortars, were turned away, but not before a number of American soldiers were hurt. I am grateful none of them died in the attack. Whatever the insurgents' purpose may have been, they also succeeded in injuring a number of prisoners. As this facility was near an Army hospital in a major city, the injured soldiers were sent there first for stabilization and surgery. Predictably, they arrived at our hospital within the next 24 hours, and each needed a careful reevaluation for changes in their condition. A few needed more surgery. One man, a medic, was injured during the confrontation. He crawled over to one of his comrades, revived him and dragged him to safety. He did this with internal injuries so severe that he ended up needing surgery and removal of a portion of his intestines. When he arrived at our facility, I could tell his medical background instantly by the terms he was using. You would not have believed that a man who had only recently awakened from an operation and had a two-foot-long incision on his belly would have no other care except to inquire about the condition of the man he saved. We noted gravely that one man's injuries were so severe he lost both of his eyes, and he had not yet awakened enough to show what damage may have been done to his brain. We checked their wounds, patched them up, and bundled them for evacuation up-range, leaving their care in the able hands of the physicians in Germany and their fates in the more able hands of God.

I have been blessed with the opportunity to meet more Iraqi children whose families seek my care, and the good fortune of commanders who graciously allow me to try and help them. They showed up at outlying bases and were sent in to me. Some have been referred by family and acquaintances, while others have been sent by Iraqi hospitals or tried us after having been turned away for being unable to pay the bill elsewhere. I met a smiling young boy with a growth on his neck. When it returned after an operation last year, the Iraqi surgeon sent him to see me. With the help of my friend, otolaryngologist Joe, I will try to remove it for good. He smiled broadly for a picture and clutched a stuffed bear donated by you good people back home.

Another baby had been unable to eat or drink due to vomiting and diarrhea, and simply required a little hydration and antibiotics to get her on her way. An Iraqi soldier came to see me with his two-week-old infant girl, and the sad story that she showed little interest in food or her surroundings. He and his wife had suffered two previous miscarriages. Their pediatrician had suggested he bring her to visit the Americans. It was immediately clear that the delicate creature in front of me was disadvantaged with a genetic abnormality. Her hands and feet were turned on their joints, and the features of her face were abnormally formed. She lay passive most of the time and only uttered a few strained, high-pitched cries. I explained to the man through an interpreter that his daughter had been born with an illness I did not think could be corrected. I told him that although I did not claim to know the future, and although when there is life there is hope, I did not think his daughter would live very long. Even if she did, she was likely to have a severe mental defect. I instructed him in some methods of getting more fluid and nutrition into her. I asked him to return on a day when there was a flight available to take a blood specimen to a lab in Germany that could confirm my suspicions. He left with my prayers, and I know his family could use yours as well.

I mentioned in March that I had met I., a girl with a diseased liver and severe yellow jaundice. After searching around for resources in Iraq, and finding only our hospital and an Army pediatric anesthesiologist at a base north of us, I committed myself to try and help her. She has a severe childhood illness causing a blockage of the liver, and it is fatal before age five if not treated. I was accustomed to treating this problem in children at two-months of age, but she was already 18-months-old and showing signs of advanced liver damage. I grappled with the fact that an operation at this late age gave her only a one-in-five chance of surviving, but compared to the zero chance of survival without surgery, both her parents and I were willing to put her through the danger of surgery. Anesthesiologist Dave, a pediatric specialist deployed to take care of combat-injured troops at another base, was very brave to accept the danger of a round-trip helicopter ride to come and help me give this little girl her slim chance of a cure. How fortuitous it was to find he was deployed to Iraq at the same time that baby came my way. I performed her operation yesterday, and I was grateful for my partner surgeon Mike's skilled and delicate assistance in getting her through it. Now that the surgery is past, I know her healing is in God's hands. I attentively monitor her progress and adjust her medications, with the good help of the nurses and physicians in our intensive care tent. Please pray for her. I have tried my best to give her a long shot. As I think another surgeon would recognize, even though her death was an eventuality without surgery, now that I have tampered with her belly I accept ownership of whatever outcome transpires.

So there you have life at Camp Balada. As the moon traverses the night sky you might ask, "What of home?" It is harder to be here than usual, tonight. As always I feel stretched; my body here and my heart anchored 7000 miles to the west. Tonight, I worry because two of our boys have not been feeling well. I know Meredith can handle it, but I also know I am not where I belong, taking care of my family. It is hard enough chasing after three boys alone, but when the burdens of nursing a sick one and making trips to the doctor are added, it's exhausting. So that is what tears me more than usual tonight. But I take comfort in something I learned in my long residency, and I hope you do, too, sweet Meredith: you can't stop the clock, and every hour brings me closer to home. Yesterday wouldn't be soon enough. If you are still there after my long ramblings, thank you for listening. I wish you warm company, chow, and bed.

God Bless,

Chris

18

"They'll Never Get My Lucky Charms!"

In 'da Camel Club
Friday, 15 APR 2005

My Dear Friends,

Good evening, how are you? I hope this letter finds you happy and well. It's actually 14 APR, but since it is 22:00, I know there is no way I will finish this letter by midnight. But since many of you are in a time zone more than seven hours later than me, I may be able to mail it to you when it is Friday here and Thursday where you are. Can you see why I can't sleep at night? It is hard to live in two time zones at once.

As the sun set tonight, I was watering my new plantings at our call room, The Swamp. Today fled by me because I slept most of the day. I was up most of last night looking after three men who came to our hospital after being injured in the north. They had all been hurt in explosions, two in an IED explosion, and one when his troop transport ran over a mine. Since the mine was actually designed to explode and hurt people, it can't rightly be called an improvised explosive device, but more of a designedly explosive device. Whatever you call it, it sucked. The injured seaman (yes, the Navy boys and girls are here too!) had fragments in the joint space of his knee, so I helped orthopedic Brian clean it out. The other men were truckers whose convoy came to a quick stop when it encountered explosions. One trucker was Filipino and the other was Jordanian. It pays well to move stuff around Iraq for the military, but the cost can be high if you are unlucky enough to drive over an IED. At least the job comes with major medical, good old Mesopotamia General Hospital here in Balad, and the G.I. doctors with the scalpel. I'm pleased to report all three gentlemen should recover well.

So after my major nap this morning AND afternoon, I rose to take care of business. In the way of an aside, it dawns on me that I haven't written in a goodly long time, specifically nine days. What that means is I might blabber on for some time here today. I even considered splitting this into two entries, but in the end decided to just write on until I ran out of steam, or it was time to get back to work. But for you reading this, maybe you might want to get a snack, a cuppa, or even visit the bathroom. And if you are at work, you might want to skip on to your important emails so my blathering doesn't keep you there all day. If you really need a break and want to have something on the screen so it looks like you are working, I'm happy to oblige.

Where was I? Oh yes, taking care of business, TCB for you Elvis fans. Once I got back from the port-a-potty, I did my errands: dump out the garbage, and drop off dirty clothes and pick up clean clothes at the Filipino laundry. Then I took my empty wastebasket, snuck over to the senior officers' hooches, and used the bin to tap off some of the water for their indoor showers to water my plants. In addition to the herbs I brought to Iraq myself, I have received a nice assortment of garden seeds from Zeta Delta Xi brother Joshua and others at home. My hooch is surrounded by a five-foot wall of sandbags, in case of any nearby mortar impact. Since the nearest beach is Basra, there isn't much sand here. The desert part of Iraq is further to the south, near Kuwait. Our ground is a gritty substance you could describe as mud, dirt, or dust, depending on how many days it has been since rainfall. Today, it was dust. Hailing from a country as young as the United States, it stretches my imagination to consider that there have been farmers, pilgrims, merchants, and soldiers trudging back and forth over this same dust between the Tigris and Euphrates Rivers for the past 7000 years or so. It makes our little occupation seem trifling.

So when you fill up a sandbag in Balad, you put in about 12 pounds of dusty tan dirt, rich with whatever washed up on these plains the last year the rivers flooded. For my plantings, I took a pick, poked holes in the sandbags, and pushed my seeds in. I feel like my home here is surrounded by not just a barrier against shrapnel, but also a near-continuous window box planter. Of course, I cut a shallow furrow at one end to plant the sunflowers, because it would have been silly to put them in the sandbags. I have been watching for five days now, and shiny tender green shoots are starting to poke their arms out of the dirt and reach for the sun. When I do my 24-hour shifts in the hospital, I give them a good soak the day before and after because the afternoon sun is brutal. Along the perimeter, I have noticed some of the farmers make little canopies over young shoots with fragments of plastic bags, so the fields look like they are full of trash, until you notice all the trash is neatly spaced in rows.

Then I armored up and went for a seven-mile jog. It was a strange jog, in that I ran three-and-one-half miles to the perimeter, jumped on the shuttle bus to get through the exposed eight miles of perimeter opposite the hospital, and then ran another three-and-one-half miles back home once the shuttle got to the more protected roads. We aren't required to wear our armor, except during an alarm red or a period of increased defense, but I have gotten so used to wearing it I feel naked outside without it. After my jog, I gathered up my Dopp kit and headed to the Cadillac shower trailer to clean up.

Before my shower, I walked the additional 50 feet to the hospital, without armor, to water the plants at The Swamp, as I started to say above. While I was pouring water from a mop bucket (slightly stinky from the diesel fuel contaminating it) over the flower boxes, I heard the call to prayer from outside the wire. The sun's orange and pink rays cut long and low across the hospital compound. As I climbed the steps to the top of The Swamp and sat on the roof looking east over the wire, across the canals and farms to the palm trees along the Tigris, I could hear the Muslim chanter's voice lilting in the evening air. Between the growl of passing Humvees and the chatter of circulating Black Hawks, his rising and falling tones reached the four miles from the loudspeakers of the mosque's tall minaret to call the faithful to evening prayers. Even though I felt naked and exposed without my armor, and visible on the roof, I lingered a few minutes to hear his chant. I don't want you to think I was taking any foolish chances sitting there; remember that practically no one wears their armor everywhere like I do, and people often climb on top of The Swamp to sip a drink or sunbathe. The brave young men and women in the guard tower between us and the wire, as well as the patrolling helicopters and Sherpa airplanes, make sure nothing sneaky is going on in the fields surrounding our base. We are well protected. I finished my watering and left the seeds to awaken to the water's kiss and the sun's warming embrace. Maybe even my muskmelons will grow.

Dinner in the DFAC had passed, so I broke out a trusty MRE. Right away I knew I was in trouble when I read "Chicken Tetrazzini". Years of punishment with soggy gobs of cafeteria turkey tetrazzini at Brown had instilled in me an aversion to the dish. But I had spent the day hibernating, and then running out all the energy my cheek pouches had stored, so it was time to eat. I cracked the steamer, activated it with water, and cooked the pouch. As I waited for it to warm, my horror was tempered by the snack in the MRE. It was one of my favorites: jalapeño cheese on wheat snack bread. I love that the snack bread has been formed in the shape of a bread slice, even though it wasn't cut from a loaf. My expectations of the main dish were precisely satisfied. The chicken chunks were uniform miniature bricks of extruded chicken by-product, and the spaghetti was fat and somehow pasty and gooey at the same time. Ah, how I miss al dente pasta. The dish was rounded out with a gelatinous, pudding-yellow, tasteless sauce, gritty with undissolved flour lumps.

Fearless reader, don't lose hope for my tender palate. As a military surgeon, I have learned to take initiative and find creative solutions. I had a bag of salt and vinegar potato chips from the DFAC, so I quickly crumbled them into the foil pouch. Better yet, I reached into my arsenal of powerful sauces and broke out the Foo's Fire. It is a treasured Louisiana-style family recipe brewed up in small batches by my friend Jerod. The Fire tastes like a tangy cayenne-based concoction. Since I have been hitting the heavy habanera stuff, I knew to pour it on in generous volume. The bright rich spark of the sauce rescued the meal, and I tucked in heartily with my trusty hobo tool spoon.

Something I have wanted to write about for some time now is the use of talismans and lucky charms by many of my brothers-and sisters-in-arms. Before coming here, I read in Anthony Swofford's book *Jarhead* how he and his fellow Marines would collect military dog tags from each deployment, modify them, paint them, and wrap them together in wads of tape. He maintained they were not just items of identification, but further, badges of experience and history. The Marines in his sniper unit would also wear a round of ammunition from their weapon around their neck. Besides identification, dog tags carry useful and personal information, like religious preference and blood type. Many of the soldiers lace one tag in their boots so medics can get to them easily and know immediately what blood type they are, should they fall in battle. Beyond their practical purpose, I find that my dog tags hang around my neck with the comforting familiarity of a religious emblem. Since I am continually scrubbing my hands for surgery, I keep my wedding band clipped into the beaded chain holding my dog tags. Also hanging here is my hooch key, since I am prone to lose anything not attached to me by flesh or metal.

Perhaps I'm superstitious, but for me it doesn't end there. In fact, if you picked me up by my ankles and shook everything off of me, quite a few talismans and lucky charms would be piled on the ground. Also around my neck are my St. Raphael and St. Barbara medals, and my "C+M=BGR" necklace. The former were a gift from my wife, and the latter was my son's idea. The initials stand for everyone in the family, and the math is quite simply the sum to which Meredith and I added up. I wear my military ID around my neck in an ID holder that also functions as a wallet or miniature man-purse. Contained therein are another collection of charms. I carry a soldier's cross loaned to me by my son's teacher. I have a photo of my three boys, my challenge coin, and the most valuable thing I brought to Iraq, Meredith's paper dollar ring. That's the ring with which I proposed to her in 1990. (Don't worry; I'm not so cheap that I haven't replaced it with a proper ring since then.)

People not in the military may not know the history of the challenge coin. The most accepted story is that a lieutenant in a World War I flying squadron had given bronze coins pressed with the unit's emblem to all his colleagues. One pilot was shot down behind enemy lines and his German captors took all his identification except the coin, which was hanging in a small leather pouch around his neck. He escaped during a nighttime bombardment, and was able to travel incognito until he reached the French front lines. The French soldiers thought he was a spy and threatened to execute him until he produced his squadron coin. Having proved his identity, they instead gave him wine and reunited him with his unit. This explains the modern use of the coin, and why it is called a challenge coin. If one member of a unit sees another in a bar, he issues a challenge by dropping or tapping his coin on the bar. If the second cannot produce a coin within a minute, he must buy the drinks. I'm not in much danger of being challenged until I leave our dry county in Iraq!

My collection doesn't end there. I keep my important papers, like orders, medical records, and Kiss Army commission in my war wallet. Also in there is my pocket flag, a dollar I received as change at Mi Tierra restaurant with John 3:16 written on it, and our family Christmas portrait with all the Coppolas dressed up like the Dalton Gang. Back in my hooch on my desk are the toys and items each of my boys gave me to hold onto during deployment. It's my job to bring them back home safely.

I may be insane in the quantity of talismans I carry, but I'm not alone in having them. Almost everyone I ask carries a little piece of home with them. It's comforting to have something familiar around the neck or in a pocket when so far from home, and with a hint of danger in the distance. Anesthetist Annie carries a ring from her husband. Anesthetist Sean keeps a picture decorated by his son on hand, and also got a really great coin from his boy. Nurse Paula wears a ring from her husband with a quote in French, which translates roughly as "to you and no other". Surgeon Todd has "Flat H." in his room. It is a life-sized traced-paper cutout of his son that came to Iraq to stay with Todd. Apparently Flat H. has done a lot of traveling around the globe, albeit folded up in a big envelope. When I asked one good friend about good luck charms, she showed me the cross tattoo on her ankle. Several weeks ago, I took a machine gunner to the operating room to remove shrapnel from his arm. He handed me a woodcut cross and asked if he could keep it with him. Roughly engraved on the back was the quote, "In all things, take my hand". I held it for him while the anesthetic began to work and then, before prepping his skin with iodine, I taped it to the palm of his right hand. We take a lot on faith, coming over here. Maybe having a little token of faith or inspiration in the pocket makes it easier to dig down and walk out there every morning to face whatever the day brings us. I know I couldn't make it through the day without the thought that there are people back home rooting for me, and someone watching over me.

As for needing a purpose to come to work, the children I get to help are more than reason enough. I told you about baby I., on whom I operated to unblock her obstructed liver. Part of the reason I have not written is that I have kept a pretty close watch on her as she recovered. I am happy to report she has made quite a lot of progress since the day I brought her from surgery to recover in Intensive Care Tent #3, accompanied by quite a crowd, but still only a portion of the many people who made her surgery possible. She must be made of pretty tough stuff, because she grew stronger and stronger each day and was even dancing with a stuffed mouse toy that played a tune and wiggled. Her appetite was excellent, and she made short work of a jar of chocolate one of the staff gave her. Her mother, continuously by her side, was happy to see her daughter perking up. She told me she wasn't at all surprised by her daughter's recovery, because "Iraqi women are strong." I was able to send baby I. and her family back home two days ago. If I do nothing else in Iraq in these 120 days, helping I. has made this trip worth the sacrifice of being here.

I've met some other children. One boy's grandfather brought him to see us because the hole he uses to pee formed in the wrong place. He yelled like a banshee while urologist Eddie and I examined him, but he was happy enough when he had his bottle back. He is strong and healthy, and the operation to repair his defect will be best performed in a year or so when he is bigger and there is a higher success rate. He will come back to Balad hospital to visit next summer, and though I can't predict the details, I have faith it will work out somehow. Perhaps even the Iraqi medical system will be back on its feet enough to take care of him. We also admitted a little girl, who had been in the local hospital for a month without getting better. She was struggling to breathe with pneumonia. Her limbs were thin with malnutrition, and contracted from disuse. When I used a needle to numb up her neck to place an intravenous catheter, she barely responded. She is now on a breathing machine and being treated with antibiotics. Her life is in danger, but where there is life, there is hope. I pray we can get her through this.

My colleagues in the hospital paid me the compliment of hanging an impromptu sign over the tent where my young patients stay, marking it as "The Coppola Hospital for the Betterment of Iraqi Children Foundation, Inc." It's a good laugh, but I hope I can live up to that challenge in some small way. One of the translators has already asked me if I would come back. Since I am committed to the Air Force for another four years, there may be a future visit to Balad in the cards.

We have had one fake but notable patient in our facility, Spec. Raghanne (a.k.a. Raggedy Anne). She has had a tumultuous past few weeks. Wild accounts abound about her valiant effort in battle and her subsequent kidnapping and captivity. A reward was offered for her captors' apprehension, and she was rescued in a daring raid. She was a little worse for wear, but I have no doubt her indomitable patriot spirit will carry her through triumphantly. The staff is naturally paying her special attentions out of admiration for her perseverance. It has been good for us to temper the stress of the hospital with a little levity.

Another patriot who visited LSA Anaconda was none other than Charlie Daniels, with his band in tow. As the sky grew dusky and the air cooler, he fiddled and sang away to do his part in showing us how much America supports her troops. When he came out on stage wearing his personalized desert camouflage uniform and his big black cowboy hat, his white hair made him look a little like Santa Claus on deployment. It was great to sit a spell, listen to good music outdoors, and in spite of the helicopters traversing the sky, imagine we were someone else. The best seats in the house were on the fire trucks and ambulances ringing the stage. Of course they were there for support in case of trouble, but it seemed like every piece of emergency equipment on base was there in the stadium. Even the military working dogs made the show. Although we were required to bring our armor and helmets, being at an outdoor concert felt just like I was home in the USA for bit. I only wish I could have had my best girl by my side.

Surprisingly, the time is flying by, and in a few weeks our detachment will be heading back home. In fact, anything mailed to me after this point probably won't make it here before I leave, so don't send anything else to me! I would hate for someone to go through the expense and trouble of sending a package, just to have it return home unopened a few months later after having made a round trip to Iraq! If you still want to send items to the troops, they can be sent to the hospital marked 'Department of Surgery', and I'll ask one of the surgeons replacing me if he will look out for packages. Before our time is gone, our group has organized to paint our emblems on the concrete barriers surrounding the hospital and helipad. Of course, not everyone could be spared from work. When you are in your climate-controlled workplace, think of our OR crew operating the bank of sterilizers as they vent steam into an already stifling tent. It is through their tireless efforts that we have clean instruments to give our wounded heroes their best chance for a successful operation without infection.

Surgeon Brian has organized what we think is the first surgical society in a deployed environment. It is the "Balad Association of Doctors Anaconda Surgical Society", but we just call it B.A.D.A.S.S. for short. As a charter member, I proudly wear my desert camouflage scrub cap with official insignia. We have had a shipment of operating room scrubs donated, and they are put to good use since we are so busy. The fabric pattern of the most recent shipment was multi-colored balls with happy faces on them. It seems a bit out of place in our combat hospital, but they do the trick when we need scrubs quickly. As we surgeons also wanted to leave our mark on Balad, we have our B.A.D.A.S.S. logo painted on the wall of The Swamp. I trust the surgeons who follow us will surpass our achievements in deed and word here at Mesopotamia General Hospital.

Well, I've gone on more than long enough. Thanks as always for reading this. As each and every one of us is an ambassador from America, I hope we are making this part of the world a little safer and better for its citizens. With a little luck, maybe any good changes we have helped to bring about will last even after we leave. Until then, we will be doing our best and clinging to thoughts and dreams of home. May the wind always be at your back and the road rise up to meet your feet.

Wishing you good fortune,

Chris

19

"Made a Difference to That One"

The Surface of the Sun
Saturday, 23 APR 2005

Dear Friends,

It's gotten hot. It's not unbearably hot, but it is earnestly hot. We've had a string of days over 100 degrees. That's not as hot as it is going to get, not by a far shot. But today, it feels like the sun is closer. It feels like it is touching. It looks bigger in the sky. Today the temperature peaked at 117. When the air is still, it feels like something palpable that parts softly in front of me as I walk. It resists movement. I can even see the heat rising off the gravel, wrinkling vision a little. When the air does move, it is a hot breeze that feels more like the heated outflow of a furnace being poured towards me like a liquid. This breeze doesn't cool. My plants are taking it hard. The newest and smallest leaves are hanging limply, and broad older leaves are yellowing and turning brittle. I've been watering more when I am able. I ran yesterday, and sweat poured off me like I'd sprung a leak somewhere under my armor. I didn't run today. We are only at three on our heat index scale that goes to five. I feel like it is already at 11.

Today went very well. Neurosurgeon Lee let me assist him in operating on a four-month-old boy with an abnormality of his spinal canal and brain. He is probably seven-months-old, but for whatever reason, his age varies with which member of his family is asked. He came with his father and some more distantly connected men, but the mother did not come. When the mother and the father disagree, I always know it is the mother who is right. In my office at home, I wait while they discuss it among themselves. They rehash memories, and review events like birthday parties and vacations. Sooner or later, a revelation dawns across the face of the father and he acquiesces to the mother's account of the dates and details. I remember it being the same with my own parents. Still, being a man, I will find myself claiming to Meredith that I remember the date better than she does. She will arch her eyebrows at me and patiently wait, until I work it out in my head and come to the realization that she had accurately remembered some detail, such as how old our boys were when we moved to Texas. It's amazing sometimes how men can be so dense.

That brings me to another fact I have found is true about caring for children. It was taught to me by one of my pediatric surgery professors at Children's National Medical Center in Washington D.C. He said, "If you haven't told the mother, you've told nobody". It's true! I could spend an hour explaining to a father every last detail of how an operation proceeded, what to expect in recovery, and how to care for a child after surgery. I could further ask him to recite it back to me, in the presence of witnesses until he has it verbatim. If the mother wasn't present, the next time I visit the child in the presence of the mother, she will start as soon as I enter the room: "What did you do to my baby?" and "This man here tried to explain it to me but he did not know." The uncomfortable father will sit behind, shrugging his shoulders and slinking back guiltily.

So until I meet the mother of this boy on whom Lee and I operated, I won't claim to know how old he actually is. His first surgery for the spina bifida defect and sac of fluid on his back was performed a week ago, and he healed quickly. He takes a bottle heartily from his father and plays actively in his bed, even though his legs do not work, like most people with spina bifida. Today's operation was to create some more space for the back of his brain. Part of his brain had actually grown too low, outside of his skull, down into the slender tube enclosed by the vertebra. It would eventually become too crowded in there, and pressure on that part of brain would interfere with his ability to keep a rhythm of breathing. Today I assisted Lee as he opened the back of the chubby little neck and cut away enough of the bottom of the skull and rigid rings of the vertebrae to give this part of the brain plenty of room. Next, we cut the hard sac surrounding the brain and spinal cord, and sewed in a patch of material from a cow's heart sac to make it wider. It was like letting out a dress with a panel of fabric for a bridesmaid who has gone beyond the waif look. With Lee's expert care, the baby did very well. It was sweet music to hear him crying and to watch him move after the anesthetic wore off, proving that he had kept all of his faculties. He will stay with us a bit more until he has healed enough to go home.

It seems like there is no end to the people who come to our hospital for care. Just now when I came home from the hospital, Lee was fixing a man's skull. It had broken in an IED attack, sending a fragment of bone into his brain. Aussie Dave, our newest surgeon, was helping him out. Upon arrival, he promptly had a B.A.D.A.S.S. cap made, individualized with a boxing kangaroo. Urologist Eddie had to help straighten someone out last night who had a "man injury". He was wearing quite an outfit, gingham operating scrub pants topped off with armor when an alarm red went off. I just admitted a three-(or five-) year-old boy who got hit by a truck. He was in good condition, with only a scrape on his head and a concussion. Luckily, children are like Bumbles, and as we know from the *Rudolph the Red-Nosed Reindeer* Christmas special, Bumbles bounce. Taking care of kids bounced off car hoods is one of the most common problems I see back home. But this steady flow of injured people makes me wonder, how can we make a difference?

We struggle along through highs and lows, but some things just take the wind out of your sails and knock you to your knees. M. is the girl I cared for when she was badly burned, but unfortunately after a month here, she died. Later that month, I took care of an Iraqi man who was shot in the belly. I operated on him twice, as did some of my partners, and I visited him day after day on rounds. He lost some intestine, he had a wound infection, and after a long slow struggle of two weeks or so, he was well enough to leave the hospital. We weren't sure if he was a local farmer or one of the insurgents. One day he would be a prisoner under guard, and the next we would receive word from security personnel that it was just a case of mistaken identity. Eventually, one of our translators, who is also an Iraqi National Guardsman, confirmed he was an insurgent who lived in the town of Balad; he routinely hijacked trucks and had even killed some of the men in our translator's unit. A few days after he went to a detention facility in this country, I learned that the man I had nursed back to health was the one who had thrown the firebomb into M.'s house. I saw red. I instantly conceived of a variety of ways I could have meted justice on him with my own hands. I've taken care of drunks who have plowed into a family of five on the highway, in the bed next to the parents whose children were killed in the crash, but nothing prior had been as difficult as this. I was thankful I didn't know who he was while he was here. I struggled with hatred for this man whose life had been in my hands, and slowly came to the resolution that the best I could do for me and for him was to pray for him. A few days later I learned that M.'s father, a soldier, was killed in action by insurgents. How will his wife rise above the loss of her daughter and her husband? I pray she finds peace.

But we do help some. The Kurdish refugee boy we cared for after he was blown up by a land mine went home to his family. He took with him two garbage bags of food he had hoarded during his recovery. I learned he was only eating a bite from his meals and saving the rest to bring to his family. You all have sent me so many good snacks and food that I made him a big care package with the items you donated. I told him he could take home the care package, but only if he would eat his meals. He went in high spirits, and had learned to take care of his colostomy. The girl who had an infection of her spinal fluid has improved. It is a wonder to me that the bone marrow specimen I took out of her hip was flown to Germany and studied in a lab, all by the hardworking men and women in the Air Force. Surgeon Todd took care of an American who was in a Humvee crash and nearly had his right arm torn off. The joint was cracked open and hanging on by a bit of muscle and skin. He and Australian orthopedic surgeon Peter worked for hours to reattach it. When he lost too much blood, the lab called for emergency blood donors. I rolled up my sleeve, and now he has a pint of Coppola in his circulation helping get oxygen to that arm.

The Americans we help are brought back to Germany, and then many are transported on to the U.S. When the patients are particularly sick, the CCAT (critical care air transport team), takes care of them. My friend anesthesiologist Bob is one of the skilled professionals who keep these sick young men alive in a flying intensive care unit, thousands of feet in the sky. Recently, neurosurgeon Todd helped transport a man with a skull tumor to Germany, and removed the tumor once they arrived. He gave me an account of the spacious interior of the cargo plane, which is converted into a hospital with wings as they fly north. It is a comfort to know that if we can keep them alive at our hospital, the CCAT team can safely get them closer to home.

You know it isn't all work here. Maybe because there is so much riding on our work, and the defeats can be so deflating, we try to play hard, too. The command staff at the hospital organized a golf tournament. Since grass is hard to come by, they had to be creative in the arena of course design. One of the skills was to drive balls down a line of empty medical equipment containers. Another was to chip into the port-a-potties.

I continue my jogs around base in my armor and helmet. I finally have earned my "Run to Baghdad" T-shirt after having run 100 miles. Many have run much further in the same time, but few have miles in armor. I dropped by the Air Force Gym to pick up my shirt with a pair of muddy shoes hanging from my vest. When we visit the gym, we are required to bring a second pair of shoes and change into them. This is left over from the spring, when there was standing water and thick mud all over the base. The mud is gone, but the rule remains, in typical military fashion. When I go the gym, I just wear my clean shoes, and carry a pair of muddy ones. I don't think I'll be asked to change into my muddy ones. Oddly enough, as my time here winds down, I have convinced another to run with me in armor. Aussie doctor Stuart is working in our ER. Back home, he is a psychiatrist, so he can claim his running with me is merely time with a mental patient. He's a good guy, and if one of us collapses from heat exhaustion, at least the other can drag the victim to the pool to be resuscitated. That is where all our runs end these days.

I've also been riding with Team Huffy Balad, my gang. The orthopedic surgeons in Team Huffy always know where the fun is. Hanging out with them, I hit the pool, the gym, and all the cool movies. We saw *Sahara* last night. It was a good update of *Indiana Jones* as a buddy movie, with the bonus of Penelope Cruz. It even had some topical tidbits, with one of the characters trying to sell black market items looted from the Iraqi Museum of History. Team Huffy also know the best meals, like when DFAC 3 is serving Indian food. Of course, wherever we go to eat, we have to first wash our hands with Fairy brand soap, as we glance at signs declaring that all food taken from the DFAC must be consumed within 30 minutes. To commemorate our band, we convened on the helipad to take a group photo, but it couldn't hold a candle to the creation made by the locals in Kang's photo shop. They were able to superimpose us on a background of Baghdad in flames. We all struck our toughest pose for the camera. Even a pacifist like me got a kick out of the picture. Truth be told, I wanted to make one from the first time I saw the display examples. I've had a flat recently, so I had to do a little repair work to get back on the road. I set up my bike behind the hospital on a pad of cement and got my hands greasy as I removed the back tire and hunted down the leak.

The end of our time here is so near that we have already celebrated with a farewell barbeque. It started with a group picture of the entire hospital staff. Our command had arranged for a Black Hawk helicopter, a Humvee ambulance, and a Bradley fighting vehicle to park on the helipad for the photo. We took several pictures, with people running in and out of the hospital to pose in shifts so there was always a small crew inside minding the sickest patients. The machines of war were imposing, and their commanders let us get a closer look, climb in, and caress the weaponry. When the Black Hawk pilot saw me near the door-mounted machine gun, I must have looked like trouble because he admonished, "Don't touch that red button!" When I climbed into the tank, my partners called it the "senator from Massachusetts pose", having some fun with me as the token liberal in the unit. I'm not the only one, but we are a rare breed in the military.

The morale area had been done up to resemble the set of *M*A*S*H*, with a sign, break-up netting, and a distance marker. As with the other ones I've seen in Balad, the distance to Hell is always marked zero miles. The barbecue was tasty, probably the best meal I've had here, and I got to apply the "Bone Suckin' Sauce" sent to me by Uncle Philly to good use. We danced, drank near-beer, and played darts and ping-pong. One by one, our commander called us up and presented us with our "Global War on Terrorism Medal". I must pause to say that I have come to this war complaining and objecting the whole way. I am still galled to be here based on hollow threats and nonexistent connections, and I see deaths of young people I believe did not have to happen in this way. I receive this medal with a heavy heart, but I accept it, because to do anything else would dishonor the men and women who are putting their lives on the line day after day over here. I'm proud of the amazing job they have done in this uncertain environment, and I'm proud that we at the hospital have been able to patch up so many and send them home alive.

I was on call during the BBQ, and the helicopters kept landing! Everyone knew the combination of a planned event and my black cloud luck while on call would guarantee a busy evening. Bouncing back and forth between the hospital and the BBQ, I took out two appendices and drained an abscess in a man's backside. One young man who had been injured in a vehicle crash had a head injury so severe there was nothing we could do to save him. As the party went on outside, we made sure he was comfortable as he quietly died. Three sick Americans stopped at our hospital on their way from another hospital in Iraq on the way to Germany. Two had head injuries severe enough that a neurosurgeon was making the entire trip to Germany with them to ensure their safety *en route*.

After the BBQ, many of the B.A.D.A.S.S. surgeons met on the roof of The Swamp to take in the night air. Two of the Iraqi translators came along. As the dusk deepened, we talked, and they told us about their thoughts for Iraq's future. One translator had previously told me how proud he is that his military unit is taking over more and more of the patrols from the Americans, and getting more adept at tracking down the insurgents. On this night, these two weren't so optimistic. M. told us how he has found Iraq to be a persistently dangerous place. He is afraid to leave the base to visit his hometown, because he has received so many death threats and has had some narrow escapes. He recently took a personal vehicle to another city to deliver some goods to a unit of Iraqi soldiers. When he approached the installation, they fired on him, crippling his car. He wasn't able to get close enough to safely clear up the misunderstanding, and hitched a ride back to the base. He expressed to us that he feels there will be a violent upheaval in the government as soon as our troops leave. One of the translators had missed work that day. These two told us his house had been hit by several rockets and burned down. He has a young pregnant wife, and we were on edge for the next two days until we learned they had escaped unharmed. I still won't stop worrying until I see him with my own eyes, and I hope he comes in to work soon. I am so appreciative of what the translators do in helping us take care of Iraqis, and I know they do it at great risk to themselves and their families.

Day after day, I try to do my best. It hurts to see and hear of the victims of war as it thrashes about. I try to embrace the victories so they can carry me through the defeats. I call home, and know I am loved and needed. This lets me get through the day. I water my plants and watch tiny things grow slowly, in such stark opposition to the precarious and indiscriminate violence that occurs. My sunflowers are reaching ambitiously for the sky, undisturbed by the infernal temperatures. A multitude of snapdragons have sprouted, even if they look a little wilted when it comes time to water them. An unknown benefactor propped up our smaller rose plant with a length of electrical cable, and it bloomed in a burst of rich pink.

In a few days, baby I., on whom I created a bypass for her congested liver, will visit my clinic. I have already heard from her father, via email in broken English, that she continues to do well. It still seems a bit mysterious to me that she and I should happen to be in Balad at the same time, and it should work out that I could operate on her. I feel like such a small speck in this war, and with little power to hamper the magnitude of death and loss around me. A friend sent me a beautiful album of family photos. In it was a starfish pin and version of a story I have heard before. Although you've probably heard it too, I'll tell it because it's on my mind tonight. Two men walked along a beach littered with starfish, washed up on the sand by the waves and baking in the hot sun. As one man paused at each step to reach down and toss a starfish back into the ocean, the other asked him, "There are so many starfish on the sand; how can you ever expect to make a difference?" The first man smiled at him, as he tossed the starfish in his hand into the water and said, "Made a difference for that one." I am thankful for you all. Rest easy and I will write again soon.

Fondly,

Chris

P.S. Please do not send anything else to me in the mail, because it probably won't make it to me in time. Thank you so much for your generous support and encouragement while I have been here.

20

"Someday This War Will Be Over And We'll Have to Go Home"

My Hooch away from Home
Monday, 4 MAY 2005

Dear Friends,

Time has a funny way of slipping by. As I type this in my hooch, I look up at these walls around me and realize this has been my home for the past 100 days or so. I realize I have taken care of hundreds of patients and done hundreds of procedures. I've been away from my family for so long, and I am filled with such a deep longing to see them again. I met new colleagues here, got to know old ones better, and grew to rely on both in times of need. It's an odd foreign routine, literally and figuratively, but I slipped into a rhythm and found my place. My stay here is much shorter than that of many others, especially those in the Army Reserve, but it has been long enough for this to feel like real life. Now that a new team is straggling in, and bits and pieces of the old team are beginning to leave, I am surprised to find things changing. It has been the same old routine day in and day out for what seems like an eternity. It doesn't seem real that the end is drawing near.

I know it has been a long time since I've written, but believe me, I've tried! Here is an abortive attempt I began two nights ago:

> It is midnight on the morning of 3 MAY. I'm on duty in the hospital, and the walls of the tent are billowing in ripples from the winds whipping across LSA Anaconda. Outside, the dust is flying in a curtain that makes it hard to see more than 10 or 20 feet in the distance. Even a trip to the outhouse has become an adventure. I donned my armor and helmet, walked outside, and secured the ER door. I had to lean forward against the wind and conceal my eyes from the flying dust just to make it the few paces to the port-a-potties. It isn't good weather for flying helicopters. Hopefully, it lets up a bit before morning so other hospitals can ship their sickest patients to us on their way home. The weather has been capricious lately. We went from 115 degree days of clear sun to off and on showers and this wind. They say the dust storms can last for days.
>
> Two days ago, something happened that pointed out how my priorities have been adjusted. I had asked a soldier to take a picture of me and the Korean doctor who was visiting our hospital. He was an internist, and he was accompanying the Korean orthopedic surgeon who was visiting our base. The orthopedic surgeon didn't speak English very well, so the internist begged to join him on the trip to serve as his translator, mostly because he wanted to see our base. As you might know, they care for a contingent of approximately 1000 Korean troops, mostly medical and support personnel, but some combat troops, in another region of Iraq. The internist had to convince the helicopter

pilot to make room by removing some equipment, but as the internist was quite small, it wasn't much of a problem. These two doctors were transporting a Korean soldier whose leg had been shattered by an IED and needed further care and evacuation back to Korea. Luckily, he wasn't worse hurt. The brave patient was a young farmer, a happy-go-lucky, friendly man who knew a few words of English like "Hey man!" and "Right on!" He was quite stoic in spite of the fact that his leg was broken in about six places. So as I showed the internist around the hospital, he wanted to take a picture with me. The orthopedic surgeon was more sanguine, and spent the time at his patient's bedside or scowling while he spoke into his satellite phone. The internist stood on tiptoes because he didn't want to seem so much shorter than me. I stood with feet apart, like I have seen my dear friend who is 6'11" do when he wants to come down to my level.

Anyway, when I handed the American soldier my camera to take the picture, he promptly dropped it on the cement walk, and little plastic shards scattered as a portion of the case cracked. In the man's defense, he was waiting in line to be seen at the ER and might have been a little lightheaded. He naturally felt bad and was concerned he might be buying a new camera. But four months of seeing people lose their legs has changed my priorities a bit, and I told him not to worry, anything can happen when there's a war on. Luckily, the camera (a Canon—I'll plug) still works just fine, even though you can see its guts a bit on one side. In the past, I might have gotten mad, but in the relative scheme of things, it just doesn't matter so much.

I've reached an interesting point in the deployment. New people are arriving and colleagues I've worked with for four months are leaving. And even though I'm surprised to find how quickly time has flown by, I'm still itching for my chance to leave. I know these days at the end are not any longer, but they seem to drag on so much more than the earlier days! Two of our surgeons, Lee and Mike, have headed home. We tried to send them off in style. Since neurosurgeon Lee has been the tireless organizer of Movie Night, we had a Movie Night in his honor and played *Napoleon Dynamite*, one of his favorite movies, yet again! If you haven't seen it, it's a movie about a misfit high school student; I laugh, but don't know why I'm laughing at something so silly. We have all memorized the lines and they pepper our conversation in the hospital. Nurse Ellen and tech Sharon even wore their hair like Deb, a character in the film with creative style. We had a great turnout, and even surgeon Todd, who always has hospital business and misses Movie Night, attended this one. This prompted him to be nicknamed "Yeti Boy", since a Todd sighting at Movie Night is rarer than seeing the Yeti.

I followed surgeon Mike around on his last day, and kept photographing him to catch his last operation at Balad. However, he kept starting new operations, even though his plane's departure time was fast approaching.

Lee and Mike have become friends of mine quickly, perhaps because of the stressful environment. I have grown to admire them both greatly, for their fine work as surgeons and the wisdom and kindness they displayed every day. It was hard to see them go, and it didn't feel right to break up the team. However, I was happy to know they were starting a journey back home to people who miss them and love them.

And the night before that, I also tried to write. I only got two lines down before I was rudely interrupted, and I had trouble going on. Now, I don't like to talk much about the alarm reds here, but that night, we had an incident within earshot of our hooches. After it passed, I checked in with the hospital to see if there had been any casualties. Fortunately, there were none. There was only one small hole in an unused building. I went back to my hooch, but I was so shaken up that I wasn't in much shape to write. I moved my mattress onto the floor and fell asleep in my armor. I rest easy knowing there are brave men out there chasing down the people doing this.

Today was a triumph of sorts. Recently, I was referred a beautiful almost-three-year-old girl who was born with a large mass on her neck. She had undergone surgery as a newborn, but this type of mass is hard to completely remove, so it slowly grew back. She had a bulge under her chin the size of two bananas, and her tongue protruded out of her mouth. She is a very bright little girl, and disliked me from the start! I'm sure it had something to do with the fact that I had to get an IV catheter into her, and it took a while to find one of her veins under her skin. My colleague, a military surgeon in another city here with whom I've worked before, asked if I could join her there for surgery, but as I needed some x-rays first (and frankly was so comfortable with my team here in Balad), I asked them to send the girl to me instead. Her parents came too, as well as a translator who was a contractor with the military. It took a lot of planning and discussion with the other team members to first get her x-rays and then operate on her. I had the fine assistance of otolaryngologist Joe, the head and neck surgeon. Our patient was very strong during the surgery, and we were able to remove most of the mass from her neck. I say it was a triumph of sorts, because I was impressed we were even able to make the surgery happen. Everyone involved pitched in to gather information and equipment appropriate to her little body. However, since I couldn't treat her tongue, I can't help but feel the work isn't finished. I'm trying to stay focused on getting her through this surgery and recovery, but my mind won't stop wandering to the future and how I'm going to get the rest done. I'm thankful to have gotten her through the surgery safely, and please pray she has a speedy recovery. Her parents were so gracious and grateful, and I could see in their faces how dearly they loved this little girl. It is a weakness of mine to have such tunnel vision that the whole world boils down the trials of one little girl. I only wish I could do more.

Not only is the crew changing, but also the environment around us. More and more plants are springing up. There are alien thorny weeds, and scrubby grass clinging to barren patches of dusty gravel. We will have a week of 110 degree sun, then the sky will cloud over and drop sudden unexpected rain on us. When the wind rushes across the base, it stirs up tall walls of dust that dim the sun and fade the view. Last week I climbed onto my hooch and watched the dust blow up and down Pennsylvania Avenue. Humvees sped off to destinations unknown, with goggled soldiers, their faces wrapped, manning the 50-gun in the turret. Two friends passed by while I was on the hooch, and of course they weren't surprised to see it was me up there. The warmth brought with it the insects. There are swarms of sand flies settling in the hospital, The Swamp, and my hooch. They are tiny green-bodied specks with delta-shaped diaphanous wings that silently lurk and bite. There is also a good supply of standard houseflies, or rather "hooch-flies", that buzz around and land annoyingly on food, faces, and wounds. I haven't been out much. I think the weather, the armor, the work, and the flies have dampened my routine. I haunt the hospital, but I try to put the time to good use. For example, I consider it a victory if I can catch someone sleeping and snap a candid photo of them. I must admit, I took a powernap on the couches outside the pharmacy this week and already three people have bragged they caught a picture of me nodding off.

I did run across one visitor to The Swamp who seemed worse off than me. A small lizard had gotten stuck in the sticky trap meant for mice. He was pretty well cemented in there, with his tail flat out behind him and his arms curled under his body at awkward angles. As I write this, I'm sure I am once again describing something in far too much detail. If I've lost you, don't worry, I understand. Anyway, even his face had gotten plastered in there, and with his one free eye he looked up at me as if to say, "Hey, Buddy, could I trouble you?" So with a little delicate work using a Q-tip and a paper clip, I had him and his tail on their way. It's not that I'm so keen on lizards. And Geico wasn't even the best deal for me. But since lizards eat bugs, I figured the enemy of my enemy is my friend. And I did feel a little solidarity with him, being stuck so ungracefully where he obviously didn't belong. Happy hunting, little dude!

We continue to try to mark the passing of seasons with some color in this taupe dustbowl. Tomorrow is Cinco de Mayo, and I thank you for your decorations! I think a Cinco de Mayo tree may be a Balad exclusive. I can't wait for Festivus! From school children, colleagues back home, and even my brother and sister-in-law, we have a good assortment of Mexican (and Ecuadorean) panache to brighten up the place. Surgeon Brett's daughter's class sent us a garland of great mustachioed chilies and burros laden with a cargo of miniature chocolate bars.

My hair has grown a bit. It grows so incredibly fast. I haven't been down to the barber shop for a "skin shave", as they call it, in a while. I'm going to get kicked out of the baldy club if I don't do something about it soon. We, the few, the proud, the bald, posed for a picture with the Bradley fighting vehicle when it visited our helipad. I think letting my hair grow is a manifestation of my yearning to get back to my other life, the one that doesn't involve Black Hawks laden with IED-wounded and patients with lice. There may very well be children with lice visiting my clinic back home, but I will treat them with pleasure just to be back in San Antonio.

Surgeon Dave showed me and surgeon Brian another tank on base which we had not discovered. It was an Iraqi model parked next to an antiaircraft gun. It looked like an antique. It was a relic from only three short years ago, but that seemed as far away as forever. This base feels like it always was and always will be ours. With the DFACs and theater, all the healthy well-fed Americans walking about, and the fine-tuned modern equipment rolling around and flying overhead, I'm impressed with the organization and presence of the best military in the world. I hope the world sees Americans for the hopeful and helpful people we are. We know we have it good, and we want to give that to the rest of the world. We may be loud, clumsy, and pushy, but everyone I talk to here wants the Iraqis to enjoy the benefits and freedoms of a democracy. Sure, I've come across a fair share of people who are ready to get home, but the men and women living and working on this base have uniformly expressed an attitude of good wishes and generosity to the Iraqis.

We are caring for a little girl who was injured in a confrontation. She was caught in the crossfire, and thankfully not mortally wounded. It must be such a frightening and uncontrolled experience for her to be swept up by our soldiers and rushed to a hospital miles from her home, without relatives, to be cared for by people who don't speak her language. She has shown remarkable spirit. It may be fear or shyness that keeps her quiet, but she has calmly regarded us, and unless she is in pain, says little and asks for little. I have seen how many of the hospital staff go out of their way to give her a smile, try to make her comfortable, or bring her a toy. This war is happening in her backyard, and I hope she can find a peaceful path through its turmoil to carry on with her life. In the short term, the good nurses and other personnel of the hospital are guiding her back to health.

We've talked about the little changes that will have to occur when we "rotate back to the world." I'm mostly stealing from surgeon Brian for these, but he just has such a good way of expressing it. I'll have to stop walking outdoors when I have to go to the bathroom. The "all clear" just sounded and I made my little trip the porta-pottie. When alarm red sounds, it is like a Pavlovian response. I always have to go pee just as the signal to stay in bunkers or armored in the hooches sounds. So after it was over I marched out to the conveniences, and walked in on someone using the loo. Unfortunately, that's what happens when you forget to lock the door, and I expect it was embarrassing for both of us. When I get home, I'll have to stop going to surgeon Todd's house at 18:30 every night for dinner. I'll have to stop getting in the hatchback of the SUV when we load up to drive to dinner. I probably shouldn't hang my wet clothes and towel on the front door after a workout when I get home. I guess there will be no more barley beverages at work, either. I'll drink the near-beer while I'm here and alcohol is forbidden, but I can't see myself stocking up on O'Douls at the HEB supermarket.

We've been here long enough that I finally got around to fixing something that has been bothering me for months. Four months before I arrived, we inherited this hospital from the Army. Everyone still calls it the "CaSH", a verbalization of the acronym CSH, which stands for Combat Support Hospital—an Army term. We are an EMEDS, which stands for expeditionary medical support hospital, and the AFTH, which stands for Air Force Theater Hospital. I think part of the problem was that the sign in front of our housing area still said U.S. Army Hospital. While having a drink with friends and watching the sunset from the 19th Hole behind the hospital, I discovered I wasn't the only one bothered by this! I resolved to fix the problem by sunrise. With some homemade stencils and a Sharpie, I had the sign shipshape in no time. Halfway through renovations, I had erased "AR" from Army Hospital and discovered "MY" hospital. It was tempting to leave it that way, but I continued. After finishing, I couldn't resist tagging the sign for the Red Tail Medics and the Balad Associated Doctors, Anaconda Surgical Society (B.A.D.A.S.S.). Within a few days, I noticed the other signs still referencing an Army hospital had been quietly remade by like-minded individuals.

So many other details stand out and are so different than home, but feel normal here. I was looking for scissors to cut off one patient's dressings. He was a Marine, and being willing, ready, and able, asked if I wanted him to help. I shrugged, "Sure". Before I could jump back, he had whipped out a five-inch blade (painted matte black for low visibility in combat) and sliced dressings off both his legs. I couldn't get my camera out fast enough.

We get a regular schedule of performer visitors to the base through the MWR entertainment division. Tonight, the Tejano group Lumbre is playing at the theater. Last night it was the rock group Hollowell. A few weeks ago, an all-girl group, The California Girls, came to play. These performers are always generous enough to visit the hospital and try to cheer the soldiers who can't make it out to their concerts. They were signing autographs and taking pictures with the troops, doing their best to lift their spirits.

As the rotation ends, there are so many rituals and events that occur. These occasions are thought provoking in many ways. It is astounding to see how the expeditionary business of the Air Force is so geared up and organized to move such a multitude of people in and out, not to mention all the equipment that goes with! A short while ago, we had a mandatory Commander's Call. "Mandatory" usually doesn't preface anything too desirable, but I was impressed to hear from each section, including our hospital's First Sergeant, what a volume of work we airmen were able to achieve in four short months. We had the B.A.D.A.S.S. charter meeting, and through the essential assistance of surgeon Brian's charming better half back home, we received quite respectable certificates for membership in a down-and-dirty league of combat surgeons.

I flew a flag over the hospital to commemorate my presence and efforts here as one man, but a man representing the greatest country on earth, even with her faults.

And lastly, to observe the birthday of the former boss of the base, the command section decorated a cake, and we got to "express our opinions" with a borrowed portrait of Saddam Hussein.

I could choose to complain about conditions, events, and the philosophy of this war. But that is not why I was sent here. I was sent to support the fighting men and women of the armed forces. Every day, I try to turn in a worthy performance. That's not all that's happened for me over here. I've also gotten the surprising opportunity to care for some children. Perhaps most significantly, I've learned a lot about myself, and what is most dear to me. It seems like I've been here forever, but it really has been a short time. Soon it will be time to go home to the woman and children I love so much, and who are my first thought on waking and my last hazy dream as I fade to sleep. And one year, sooner or later, all of America's sons and daughters in the military will board transports and leave this place. Someday this war will be over, and we'll all have to go home.

American and proud,

Chris

21

"Spent Ammunition"

Limbo, Iraq
Thursday, 12 MAY 2005

Dear Friends,

I've become a squatter. For the past few days, I have been living in surgeon Todd's hooch, my gear in the corner, folding out a cot each night after we finish watching movies. Days are a goat rope of wake, wash, eat, wait, eat, wait, eat, wait, and sleep. Our replacements are here, work carries on in the hospital, but our little group of surgeons has yet to leave. We linger on in Balad and wait, and wait. As each plane passes overhead, we stare at it longingly and reassure each other, tomorrow we will be on a plane out of here.

The changeover at the hospital, and at the other Air Force facilities, has been a beehive of activity with people coming and going. Everywhere I look, there are strangers working in the hospital. I walked through the emergency room the other day, and didn't recognize a face. Of course there are a few arriving from my home station, bringing news of business back in San Antonio. It just makes me long for home all the more. I've enjoyed seeing people from each specialty leading around their replacements, introducing them to the tricks of the trade. And orthopedic Brian is suddenly bigger than Jerry Lewis in France. He has a duo of French documentary producers wiring him for sound, and following him through operations and Karaoke performances.

The new surgeons have taken over admirably. We have effectively passed the torch, or at least our ceremonial B.A.D.A.S.S. mace. The mace is an ornate and decorated plunger bearing a complicated wound dressing. This new team has weathered a few rough nights. With the recent offensive against the insurgents, we were provided with an unfortunate busy period, but this gave ample chance to challenge and train the new group. It brought back memories of my first few nights on call. The first night I was on call, months ago, the medics brought in an Iraqi policeman who had been shot in the belly and was bleeding to death. I was alert, excited, and moving a mile a minute as I identified the source of the bleeding and positioned the tissues for repair. Surgeon Steve, who was on his way out, was relaxed and nonchalant as we worked together to keep the man alive. After three months in the hospital, and many operations, we released this man to an uncertain fate in one of the Iraqi hospitals. They are so busy, yet still understaffed and short on supplies. The doctors and local governments are struggling to rebuild them, all under the pressure of so many community and infrastructure challenges. Then last week, after a month with no news, the man came back. He was looking better and had a well-groomed beard. He was still too skinny, but standing on his own two feet, smiling and strong. His healthy presence cleared a question from my mind and reinforced that we had done something good here. Without surgeon Steve and the rest of our hospital, that man would be in a grave. His life is a testament to what we achieved.

I've gotten to catch up with many of the kids we treated in the past few weeks. The girl with the neck mass flew back to her hometown. Her parents were thankful and hopeful the work we did would ensure a future without her neck and tongue mass suffocating her. I got to check up on the baby on whom neurosurgeon Lee and I closed a hole in the back of his spine, and opened up the back of his skull to make more room for his brain. He was active and happy. Cardiologist Kirk, a friend from home who takes care of children, helped me examine and diagnose an infant with congenital heart disease. The boy's abnormal heart was struggling to get enough oxygen to his tissues, turning his lips blue whenever he cried. His heart defect was complicated and could not be easily fixed, but we sent his mother home with our prayers and good wishes that he grow a little older and larger so at some point in the future he could undergo corrective surgery. His will was strong enough to survive five months out of the hospital without doctors or surgeons, so I think he will make it. His mother cried, but then strengthened, thanked us, and tenderly carried her baby home. The girl who got caught in the crossfire finally took her first tentative steps after three operations on her leg. At her bedside, surgeon Todd, whom I've seen delicately rebuild fine blood vessels, fumbled as he tried to teach her how to load a PEZ dispenser. A teenager on whom I had fixed a hernia asked me to take a picture of her with her mother. You could see the divide between generations in their faces, clothes, and mannerisms. Under all that, the smile was the same. The young lady communicated in broken English her mother's insistence that I print a copy of the picture for her. I also got to see I., the girl with the liver disease, one more time. She had weathered the first month at home well, but required a few adjustments of her medications. I'm grateful that Aussie surgeon David, who is staying a bit longer than I am, has agreed to check on her progress for me. One other boy, A., whom I treated for a problem with his bottom, was doing well and looked happy. His father said he had seen no problems, but the boy complained of a few residual difficulties. His father gently interrupted and told me he thought his son was making up some minor problems just to have an excuse to come back to the hospital!

With the new staff arrivals, the hospital was changing under our feet. We tried to leave our mark and show we had laid out a slice of our lives here. The departing surgeons left their OR shoes, covered in dried blood from countless emergent operations, on display in the 19th Hole. The 19th Hole is a little oasis of relaxation tucked behind the command section of the hospital. It's a great place to take a load off, sit under the break-up netting, and watch the sunset. As the sky blazes orange and pink, the shadows grow long and stretch across the gravel and dust on the hospital compound. We sit out there, sip a near-beer, and enjoy a snack. The talk sometimes stretches long into the darkness. We may be departing the 19th Hole, but our names are written on the wall, where they will watch over those who follow in our place.

We are not the only ones. A friend in the pharmacy inked an impressive cartoon mural on the wooden walls of the corridor leading to her section. Each of the pharmacy staff was depicted as a cartoon hero saving Balad.

It's not too bad a time to leave. As I was departing the hospital late one night, I glanced up and saw something orbiting the fluorescent tube illuminating the entrance. Actually, I saw thousands of little things: sand flies. They swarmed around the light in a cloud of dancing motes. At night while we sleep, they mercilessly feast on us. They are tiny little beasts, with pale green bodies and tiny clear wings, difficult to see on the attack. We awake with itchy little bites on any exposed skin, and I mean any exposed skin. We spray DEET and spread permethrin, but the best defense I've found is to crank the air conditioner to high, and bulk up on covers. The cold temperatures seem to curdle their insect blood and slow them until they sink to the floor and become vulnerable targets.

My sunflowers continue to spread lush green leaves and extend thick healthy stems skyward. Tiny black ants busy themselves with climbing up and down, seeking a few drops of water or food at the base of the leaves. I gave a few of my plants away. Since most of them are in sandbags, it was as easy as carrying the sandbag to a friend's hooch. There is a hint of rain in the wind today, so perhaps they will drink well.

When we pass through the hospital, people ask us, "Are you still here?", or "When does your plane leave?" I'd sure love to know! Trouble is, once your deployment is over, you are low priority. Last winter, our commander gathered us for an information session with our families. He said we would be over there in a hurry, but the ride home was a little different. Once your work is done, you are like spent ammunition. You no longer have anywhere to be, or have much use to the military. They will get you home, but they will take their sweet time about it. Lots of people and equipment have to move, and redeployment home is about last on the list. Soldiers and equipment have to get to the battlefield. Injured troops need to be transported out of theater for further care. People with family emergencies at home need to be rushed out, too. Service members taking short trips to complete training need to get somewhere and back on a schedule. And behind all of these, we wait, and wait, and wait.

As I wind bored circles around the base that has been my home for four months, I notice little details that would have stood out as strange before my time here. Someday, perhaps not right away, I'll miss some things about this place, so I'm trying to capture the details, both good and bad. There are strict requirements at the post office, and countless signs, one of which says redundantly, "Read signs". My post office back home doesn't have an amnesty box in which to drop guns and ammo you might have been tempted to sneak into a package. At the pool, there are the old standby rules, but also included are rules forbidding firearms, and swimmers with recent smallpox vaccination. In my neighborhood, you can find a tank on the street corner.

Landscaping projects, such as a horseshoe pit, are readily accomplished with a few sandbags, which are always in abundant supply. And in our OR, if the lights go out, as they often do, we just flip on an electric torch and get right back to it.

We leave with our heads full of memories and our hands full of experience. We are confident in the able troops taking over the hospital. As the days go by, with too much time on our hands, the longing for the sweet faces of home grows even stronger, if possible. Many have passed through our operating rooms, and we have poured our hearts into our work day after day. And now in the parlance of the military, it's time to hurry up and wait. We may be spent ammunition, but we leave secure in the knowledge that we hit the mark.

Peace and happy days,

Chris

22

"Just Trow Numbers"

Hearth and Home, USA
Wednesday, 17 MAY 2005

Dear Friends,

Home is such a flood of emotions and experiences, all good. Of course it has been a whirlwind, and it has been hard to find time to sit down, much less write. Finally my insane sleep habits work out well for me. With jet lag, I feel tired every night at 19:00 and wake up at 04:00. That's a schedule I can use! Last night I stayed up until 22:00, trying to shake off the last lingering tastes of the DFAC through dinner with Meredith at Biga on the Banks restaurant. We sat at our table overlooking the Riverwalk, and staring into her beautiful blue eyes two feet away after a separation of 7000 miles was heaven. Funny, the tricks of the mind—it seems like I was hardly gone for an instant, now that I'm back. As a humid sky over the circling water taxis and dinner boats darkened, Victor brought us our food, fresh and delicious, on real ceramic plates. A grapefruit martini and a mojito paved the way for appetizers of tempura shrimp over ginger, soy noodles, and mint; next came packets of ground game meats with peanuts wrapped in crunchy fresh radicchio leaves. The meat course of tenderloin and veal chop was a delight of rare succulent cuts. Dessert, of course, was slush and ice cream at Sonic, served by a high school carhop on roller skates.

But the numbers on the calendar have peeled away quickly since Friday the 13th; when I was cramped in the Space Available terminal at Balad, watching yet another flight home slip through our fingers as it was converted to a medical evacuation flight. We're doctors, we protested, we would work on the medevac flight if they would let us on! By this point, we had been joined by chief of staff George, operations officer Tim, orthopedic Rick, anesthesiologist Marc, and others from the hospital. We all were taking our chances, trying to squeeze into the available passenger seats on the sporadic flights leaving Balad for Germany. The counter clerks knew us all by sight and name at this point. For each flight that came up, they told us we were top of the list; we had already been manifested as passengers. Then circumstances would conspire against us to snatch the flight back as it was turned into a troop movement, medevac, or Special Forces flight.

We had watched every movie in the hooch in which we had any fading interest. We rehashed the *Matrix oeuvre*. Fashion TV, our traditional pre-dinner entertainment, was mainly showing reruns of shows we had seen two and three times before. Each time we clomped back into the Space A. terminal, I wished I were a goldfish. If I were a goldfish, with a memory span of only eight seconds, I could enter that far too familiar terminal and say, "I've never been here before". Each time new trauma czar Brian left for the hospital, he would look us over with a generous and sympathetic smile as we crammed our luggage and bodies into one side of his hooch. People at the hospital, when they caught a rare glimpse of us, would echo "Still here?", and "Didn't catch the plane, huh?" These were well-meaning yet frustrating questions. On Thursday, 50-knot winds across the runway and a dust storm sweeping in threatened to ground all flights and brought into question whether (weather?) higher powers had designs to keep us in Iraq. Surgeon Todd wrapped a bandanna around his face deep-desert style and led us to and from the terminal.

As we crossed midnight on Friday the 13th, our numbers came up and we were booked on a flight. Then the announcement came: "The flight to Germany has changed". Not again! The flight was diverted to Kuwait to pick up HR before we traveled onto Germany. Did we still want the flight? Absolutely! But what is HR? Human remains. We would be traveling with the honored dead. This tempered our joy in going home, knowing some of our fellow passengers would be going home in a box. Suddenly, the inconveniences of the past three days didn't seem quite so bad. Our fallen comrades were catching an early flight back to the USA; I was more than satisfied to be traveling a few days late and alive. As we were soberly mulling this over, we were startled out of a reverie by four explosions in quick succession, loud enough to be a controlled detonation, or close by if it truly was an attack. The alarm red siren gave us our answer, and we all filed out of the terminal into the cramped concrete bunker behind the tent. Yes, even the Space A. terminal was a tent. Many troops had hopes to get on that flight, so we found ourselves crammed three abreast in the narrow bunker. I can reach out and touch each wall, and my head touches the ceiling, to give you an idea of how big (or rather, small) it is. Claustrophobia, anyone? We settled into the darkness and I passed around a pack of gum. For the first time during an alarm red, I was without armor, as it was packed into my nearly coffin-sized rolling trunk just outside the terminal. We joked and heard from other troops what their bases had been like. We heard on the portable radios the proximity of the impact site. I wondered if the insurgents themselves had plans to delay our departure from the country. Soon enough, the "all clear" sounded, and we shuffled back into the terminal.

We were all called out to march baggage around to customs and prepare for the flight. This was new! We dragged our heavy bags of personal and military gear into a plywood chute to have their contents inspected. Everyone got a chance to pass through the amnesty booth alone, and throw their illegal weapons and contraband into a hopper if they had second thoughts about sneaking them out of the country. I had no donation for the plate. The Navy customs official removed layer after layer of clothing and gear from my one piece of luggage, the oversized trunk. I somehow got it packed back in. Outside again in the gravel lounge, we watched our luggage being wrapped and netted into eight-foot-tall pallet cubes for transport to the airplane on a fork lift. We passed around my satellite phone to send cautiously optimistic messages home. The week before, a colonel told us he had gotten as far as the runway, actually laid eyes on the plane, and was turned back when the mission was converted. We calculated our arrival in Germany and began finagling a commercial flight home with various airline operators.

The C-17 is a versatile cargo hold with wings. Human cargo is almost an afterthought, with a row of spartan jump seats down each side of the plane. There are no windows but the small portholes on the emergency doors. Passengers face inward toward the cargo. The interior is wide and tall, and the back of the plane opens as a ramp that lowers to the runway so pallets of cargo can be rolled in and out. A bus could drive into the cargo bay from the rear. After the loads had been stored (our luggage and several pallets which contained stacks of pallet bottoms), we filed into the narrow aisles that remained on either side and strapped into our seats. The walls were uncovered and functional with myriad cables, wires, and hoses running to and fro across every surface. The roar of the four jet engines was a continual and almost palpable presence. We all wore earplugs, and conversation was impossible but for hand gestures and mouthed words. As the hydraulics lifted the aft ramp shut, our last view of the darkened and dusty runway of Balad narrowed into a sliver, and disappeared.

Thus began 32 hours of travel, all on Friday the 13th. As we moved west, chasing the sun into earlier and earlier time zones, we stretched out our day. I can't think of a luckier number than 13. The day I get to head home is a good one. Anyone who plays craps knows that an unlucky number in one situation is a lucky one in another. My friend Vone, who taught me how to play, told me the story of a couple in Vegas, the man teaching his wife how to play craps. Each time she would roll the dice, she would ask him, "What number should I get?" He'd reply, "Don't think about it, baby, just trow numbers." That's how it goes; you can't control what number comes up, but sooner or later, you get a good one.

Kuwait dawned hot and dry as the ramp opened. In the terminal, we watched a hopeful Spurs game, but found out later it didn't turn out so well. A grinder at the Subway trailer on the side of the runway tasted great because it was something different and a taste of home. Back on the plane, the cargo was replaced with four flag-draped coffins, plain rectangular metal shipping containers. We quietly filed in on either side of the fallen soldiers and took our seats. Now, the massive cargo bay seemed bigger and emptier. Without the pallets of cargo between us we could see each other across the hold, over the coffins. Faces were grim and contemplative. We took off without conversation.

At altitude, the pilot let us stretch our legs and take advantage of the empty space. Some slept; some read books, or listened to music. Like others, I stretched a sleep roll on the metal grid of the cargo bay floor and lay down with my head on a crumpled towel. To one side of my head were the boots of another resting troop, and to the other, I was face to face with the American flag draping one of the HR containers. I thought about the reception I would receive upon returning home, and the sad homecoming awaiting these dead men beside me. I knew how fortunate I was to have made it that far safely, and I hoped our little corps could escort these men with honor and dignity. It was humbling and saddening to bear witness to those who had paid such a horrible price in this war. I counted my blessings and said a prayer for their families, though I can't imagine their loss.

Germany was greener and somehow more familiar than the desert around the airbase in Kuwait. Volunteer Celeste in the USO office was a warm smile and a friendly face. She provided a DSN phone for calling home and a comfy couch on which to rest. The cafeteria was closed (it was 17:00, and dinner didn't start until 20:00 in Germany), so Celeste gave us some packages of cookies. There were a few seats available on a flight departing soon for Dover, DE, so we rushed our baggage onto the conveyer belt and boarded, continuing our Friday the 13th journey. The four coffins were joined by a fifth, and the passengers now included a family of five, making use of space available travel to visit home from their station in Germany. Seeing an American family made home seem closer. Dover was perfect, because a midnight shuttle ride brought me to the warm hospitality of my mother-and father-in-law in Maryland. They tucked me into the lighthouse-decorated room my son uses when he visits them. There was even a "Welcome Home" sign waiting for me on the first soft bed I'd used in four months.

Words can't describe how wonderful it was to embrace Meredith again. It was a dream come true, and as we squeezed each other tightly at the terminal in San Antonio, I thought I would never let go. The boys were a wild joy, and in the short time I had been gone looked a little bigger and somehow more mature. Our youngest had turned two and was talking much more than when I left. On the drive home from the airport, he kept saying "Daddy!" over and over again to each of us, in case anyone had forgotten I was home. There were more homecomings; the neighborhood, my son's school, and of course a nice military checklist to fill out at work! However, I made short work of that and was happy to start the two weeks of reconstitution time allotted for me to rest and recharge before getting back to business at the hospital. As I walked around, I was struck again and again by how green everything was. Grass and trees and even the moisture in the air were welcome and familiar. I was happy to be wearing the green, not tan, battle dress uniform once again.

Though home is so familiar and comfortable, practically unchanged, it is hard to know if I can fully appreciate how I've changed. If it's possible, I feel like I look upon my family with a deeper love and appreciation, because I know I have been given a gift to have come home to them safely. I don't want to let them out of my sight, and it will be hard when the day comes to go back to work! I think of friends left behind in Balad and those whose lives have touched mine irrevocably. My labors there may have been steady and perhaps even difficult on occasion, but I feel like I have been given so much more in experience than I was able to give of myself. I'll never forget the people I treated, nor the ones whom I couldn't save. I can't help but feel there is more to do, but for the moment that duty rests on the shoulders of our courageous and able replacements. Even today, there are reports of bombings and mass graves in the news. I know as I write in the comfort and safety of my home, there are still many Americans in harm's way. I pray for the day to come quickly when there is peace, and they can come home to their families. I wonder how it is that I have been so fortunate to have the privilege to care for those in need in such a dangerous place, and then to come home safe and sound to my wonderful family. I guess I'll stop thinking about it and "just trow numbers". Stay safe, love life, and have fun.

With warm friendship,

Chris

Epilogue

Little girl I., who underwent surgery to bypass her congested liver, continues to do well months after her surgery. However, blood tests show that her liver failure will recur and she will need a liver transplant in the future if she is to survive. The little girl who underwent removal of a neck mass returned to her hometown. The U.S. Army surgical commander in the area was able to locate a specialist skilled in a technique called radiofrequency ablation, and she is receiving treatments to shrink her enlarged tongue. Baby A., who was transported by helicopter to another facility for treatment of his leishmaniasis, later died from complications of his infection. The Air Force Theater Hospital in Balad continues to be busy and is staffed by a new complement of dedicated and skillful American and

Australian medical personnel. Next to Hooch A9, a six-foot-tall sunflower towers defiantly over the sandbags, dust, and gravel.

978-0-595-36624-8
0-595-36624-4